Breed Stan
Staffordshire

COLOUR
Red, fawn, white, black or blue, or any one of these colours with white. Any shade of brindle or any shade of brindle with white. Black and tan or liver colour highly undesirable.

SIZE
Desirable height at withers 35.5 to 40.5 cms (14 to 16 ins), these heights being related to the weights. Weight: dogs: 12.7 to 17 kgs (28 to 38 lbs); bitches 11 to 15.4 kgs (24 to 34 lbs).

TAIL
Medium length, low set, tapering to a point and carried rather low. Should not curl much and may be likened to an old-fashioned pump handle.

HINDQUARTERS
Well muscled, hocks well let down with stifles well bent. Legs parallel when viewed from behind.

FEET
Well padded, strong and of medium size. Nails black in solid coloured dogs.

COAT
Smooth, short and close.

BODY
Close-coupled, with level topline, wide front, deep brisket, well sprung ribs; muscular and well defined.

Staffordshire Bull Terrier

◇

by Jane Hogg Frome

9

Table of Contents

23

31

35

61

DISTRIBUTED BY:
INTERPET
P U B L I S H I N G
Vincent Lane, Dorking
Surrey RH4 3YX
England

Copyright © 1999, 2003 Animalia Books S. L.
Cover design patent: US 6,435,559 B2
Printed in South Korea.

Photo Credits:

Norvia Behling
Carolina Biological Supply
Kent and Donna Dannen
Wil de Veer
Doskocil
Isabelle Francais
Tony George
James Hayden-Yoav
James R. Hayden, RBP

Dwight R. Kuhn
Dr. Dennis Kunkel
Mikki Pet Products
Phototake
Jean Claude Revy
Nikki Sussman
Theo von Sambeek
C. James Webb

Illustrations by Renée Low

ORIGINS OF THE
Staffordshire Bull Terrier

Mankind has enjoyed the faithfulness of the dog by his side for centuries. Few dogs desire to please their human masters as much as the Staffordshire Bull Terrier. Dogs in general have accommodated man and his every whim for many generations—anything to please the master. Today's Staffordshire Bull Terrier, in mind and body, echoes that sentiment with might and determination.

A SPECIALIST IN BODY AND MIND

Before the days of dog shows and the purebred mating of champions, humans recognised the merit in dogs that could specialise in performing a specific job or task. We bred dogs that could hunt, herd, haul, guard, run, track and perform countless other tasks geared toward making our human lives more comfortable, enjoyable, and manageable. Each dog's

(opposite page) A bold metaphor of Britain's spirit, the Staffordshire Bull Terrier represents the modern example of the bull and terrier dogs. This muscular beauty is called Wildstaff Nightmare.

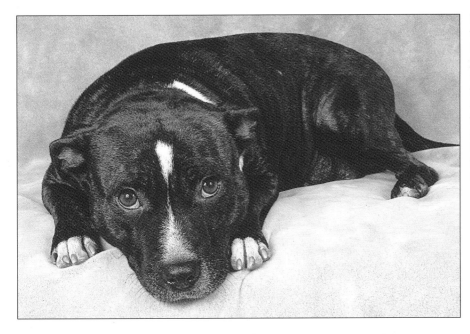

Understanding the Staffordshire Bull Terrier as a pet requires knowledge of the dog's history as a baiting and fighting dog. No dog matches this breed's devotion to its master, in mind and body.

DID YOU KNOW?

Since dogs have been inbred for centuries, their physical and mental characteristics are constantly being changed to suit man's desires for hunting, retrieving, scenting, guarding, and warming their master's laps. During the past 150 years, dogs have been judged according to physical character-istics as well as functional abilities. Few breeds can boast a genuine balance between physique, working ability and temperament.

The characteristics of a fighting dog still distinguish the Staffordshire Bull Terrier, including the pronounced cheek muscles, long legs and loose shoulders.

anatomy reflected the tasks that men set before him. The hunting dog had an insulated coat, a super-sensitive nose, a short-coupled body, a deep chest and straight, strong legs. The coursing dog had longer legs, a tucked-up abdomen (for speed), a deep chest (for lung capacity), keen eyesight, and a narrow, long muzzle (to slice the wind). The guard dogs were true heavyweights: massive and solidly boned with punishing jaws and nerves of steel.

The physical characteristics that set apart the Staffordshire Bull Terrier are its impressive muscula-ture, its strongly undershot strong jaws and large teeth, very pronounced cheek muscles, loose shoulders, roach back, low-slung body and long legs that bend in the forequarters. These are the characteristics of a fighting or baiting dog that enable it to

perform the tasks that the breed, indeed all the bull and terrier dogs, were created to tackle. The decree 'Go low, pin and hold!' was in sooth a battle cry! This imposing physique was needed for the dogs to fight one another, as well as to dodge and grab an ornery bull with their powerful gripping jaws and hold on to it without being tossed aside!

Baiting a bull, an animal twenty or more times the size of a dog, placed some obvious demands on the dog, its anatomy and tempera-ment. The desired temperament of a bull and terrier dog for baiting was not a vicious, risk-taking daredevil. Instead, the baiting dog required an even-keeled, level-headed, obedient

Although the Staffordshire Bull Terrier today doesn't pursue wild game, like boar and bear, as its ancestors did, the American Bulldog is still used on these risky pursuits.

temperament, peppered with patience, indomitable courage and tenacity. The bulldog excelled in the pinning and holding of a bull, but lacked the flexibility required in the dog pit. Thus, the smaller bull and terrier dogs were designed to take on this challenge and each other.

DID YOU KNOW?
Dogs and wolves are members of the genus *Canis*. Wolves are known scientifically as *Canis lupus* while dogs are known as *Canis domesticus*. Dogs and wolves are known to interbreed. The term canine derives from the Latin derived word *Canis*. The term dog has no scientific basis but has been used for thousands of years.

Imagine the heart of the dog that willingly undertakes such a task for the sake of pleasing his master! Baiting and fighting dogs were not the only kinds of dogs that risked their lives for their human counterparts. Indeed, herding and droving dogs, big-game hunting dogs, and even the smaller terriers risked their lives for the sake of accomplishing their tasks. Nonetheless, the bloody endeavour of slaying a bull overshadows almost any other task set before a dog.

The original fighting dog types were large, mastiff dogs with heavy, low-slung bodies and powerfully developed heads. Some accounts also describe the deep,

The American Staffordshire Terrier, shown here, derived from the Staffordshire Bull Terrier from crosses to other terriers in the U.S.

frightening voice of the mastiffs. In appearance, the mastiffs were appalling and frightful. Mastiff dogs yielded not only fighting dogs but also flock guards, scenthounds and other powerful hunters. Consider the size and fearlessness of such modern-day mastiffs as the Great Pyrenees, Kuvasz, Dogo Argentino and Spanish Mastiff. Consider the size and features of the Bloodhound, Great Dane, Newfoundland and Polish Hound. All these dogs derive from crosses to these powerful mastiffs of yesteryear.

ORIGINAL PURPOSES OF THE GREAT MASTIFFS
Historians have recorded many impressive duties amongst the purposes of these original mastiffs. Dogs used for war—armoured, spiked, and collared—became

Three modern-day breeds that derive from similar mastiff heritage: The Spanish Mastiff (upper left), shown here as an adolescent, is a powerful guard dog that can weigh three or four times a Staffordshire. The Dogo Argentino (upper right) has been called 'a huge pit bull,' developed in Argentina to hunt large game. The Polish Hound (bottom) is a large scent-hound with obvious mastiff influence.

13

The elegant but fearless Kuvasz is a flock guardian that bears no resemblance to the Staffordshire but derives from ancient mastiff stock.

(opposite page) Detail from 'Patio de Caballos de la Plaza de Toros de Madrid,' by Manuel Castellanos, a Spanish painting from 1853, shows the ancient mastiffs, resembling a crude version of our English Mastiffs today. These large, heavy dogs were used for animal baiting and warring. (Museo del Prado, Madrid)

valuable weapons for humans trying to defend themselves from their enemies. These dogs were not only brave but aggressive and resourceful. As early as 2100 B.C. dogs were employed for warring purposes. Many famous kings and tribes used dogs to claim their victories. The dogs were trained in combat and were uniformed with impenetrable metal shields and spiked collars to protect them from their foes who carried spears and other primitive weapons. Spanning the millennia, Hammurabi, Kambyses, Varius, and Henry VII were among the monarchs that valued dogs in their militia. These dogs were necessarily vicious and trusted no one except their one master. Appropriately these war dogs were labelled *Canis bellicosus*.

The great mastiffs also assisted man by hunting large, ferocious game. These dogs commonly

hunted in packs, maintained by the royals, and were used to pursue bison and aurochs in the wild forests. Dogs were also used to track the stag, considered a noble game, as well as the wild boar, the most dangerous of wild game, revered for its ruthless, nasty disposition. The mastiffs worked in conjunction with lighter, swifter dogs that tired the boar before the mighty mastiffs were released to slay it. Many men, dogs and horses were killed by wild boars fighting for their lives. There are accounts of boar dogs being kept in kennels 6000 dogs strong. Today, mastiffs are rarely used for these purposes, but there are still boar hunts in the U.S., Germany and the Czech Republic.

Bear hunting, even more popular today than boar hunting, was also a noble pursuit of the dogs of antiquity. The dogs were required to track the bear, corner it and keep it occupied until the hunters arrived with their firearms. The bear is a highly intelligent creature that could weigh as much as 350 kgs and could easily outmatch a dog. Mastiffs in India produce the most colourful tales of hunting, including the pursuit of buffalo, leopards, panthers and elephants! Regardless of the actual truth of many of these accounts, the stories underscore the fearless tenacity of these mastiff dogs that are the ancestors of our Staffordshire Bull Terrier.

Although the English Bulldog contributed to the composition of the bull and terrier dogs, today's Bulldog bears little resemblance to his nineteenth-century ancestors.

THE BULL AND TERRIER CROSS

The term 'bull and terrier' refers to a common cross between bulldog types and the smaller terriers. Bulldogs during the mid-nineteenth century did not resemble the jolly English Bulldog that we know and love today. These dogs more resembled the taller, longer-headed dogs that we recognise as American Staffordshire Terriers or pit bulls. Experts purport that the terriers used were likely the Black and Tan Terrier, the progenitor of the Manchester Terrier of today, or perhaps the White English Terrier, a breed extinct in its

original form but the forefather of the modern Bull Terrier. These original bull and terrier crosses were desirable to create the smaller, agile and fearless canine needed for the 'sport' of dog fighting. The larger mastiffs, while brave and heroic in battle and big-game hunting, were less successful in the pit. Unless a dog was suitably small, swift and flexible enough, it could not manoeuvre its way about a charging bull or another canine opponent. This is an age-old lesson that tends to evade many bulldog fanciers, especially Americans who always insist that bigger is better. Even in the U.S. today there are strains of American Pit Bull Terriers that are so large and awkward that they exceed 120 pounds. The question of size in the Staffordshire Bull Terrier would continue to be an issue for many years.

The Bloodhound is the heaviest of the modern-day scenthounds and possesses an evident mastiff heritage.

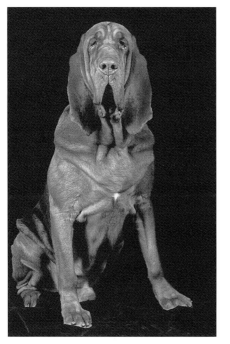

The Staffordshire Terrier's forefathers were the companions of the working class in the 'Black Country' in Stafford. In this part of England, bull and terriers were bred with great intensity and owners continued to match their dogs in the pit long after dog fights were outlawed. Hardcore Staffords believed that the dog pit was the only true test of their dogs' worth and perceived these matches as 'working tests' to determine which dogs were worthy of being bred. This mentality corresponds note for note with the show world's perspective of using the show ring to determine which dogs should be bred. Making up a champion in the show world is

assuredly a challenge, and only those dogs that prove themselves in the show ring deserve to be bred. Likewise, though obviously more lethal a game, the Staffords used the dog pit to determine who the 'champions' were, so that only the 'gamest' dogs of all would produce the next generation of fighting dogs.

The term 'game' applies to the most desirable attribute of a bull and terrier. Gameness indicates that the dog will fight fearlessly to the death and never think of quitting. It is this tenacity for which breeders strived in their bull and terriers. Likewise, game-bred pit bulls today are still tested in the pit despite the illegality and the risks involved. Dog fighters employ the terminology 'scratch' to indicate how many times in a fight a dog cowers or tries to exit the pit.

The American Pit Bull Terrier embodies many of the same characteristics as the Staffordshire. Many breeders in the U.S. breed Pit Bulls that are overly large and awkward.

DID YOU KNOW?

The bull and terrier cross, regarded as a breed by some, was sometimes called Half and Halfs. This nickname reflects the combination of the bulldog and terriers that was used to create this type of dog. As time went on, fanciers argued over the desired proportion of bull and terrier in the breed. The Staffordshire Bull Terrier has considerably more bulldog in it than does the Bull Terrier or American Staffordshire Terrier, though the relationship between all these dogs is evident.

THE STAFFORDSHIRE TERRIER
Not until the 1930s did fanciers attempt to establish the Staffordshire Terrier as a separate breed and begin to imagine their dogs competing outside the dog pit. While dog fighting was outlawed before this time, fights were still routinely held in a more or less clandestine fashion. It was around this time that the dog-fighting activities were actually abolished through police intervention, and by 1930 the law began to be fully enforced.

For the sake of establishing the breed and entering dog show, the original standard, based on the superb show winner Jim The Dandy, owned by Jack Barnard, was drafted by the very committed breeder Joe Dunn. It was adopted in 1935 at the first meeting of the Staffordshire Bull Terrier Club. It was subsequently recognised by The Kennel Club later that year, and the breed was allowed to enter dog shows. The original club was established by more than 40

breeders and Jack Barnard was the first president. The dogs were first shown at the Hertfordshire Agriculture Society in June of 1935, just one month after the club's establishment. The following year, Cross Guns Johnson, owned by Joe Dunn, won the class at Crufts Dog Show, the first time the Staffordshire had entered. Gentleman Jim was the first champion with The Kennel Club, who won his first Challenge Certificate at the Birmingham National Show. He made up his championship in double time—in just two shows! The first championship show for Staffordshires, held by the Southern Counties Staffordshire Bull Terrier Society, attracted 300 dogs in June of 1946.

The pioneers of the breed, who lived in the Black Country, were not pleased with the entrance of the Staffordshire into the show world. They feared that the temperament of the breed would be endangered and that the true heart of the breed would be lost. Many of these pioneers continued to fight their game Staffordshires to keep the 'heart' in their blood. Another controversy emerged concerning the desired size of the dogs. In the original standard, the size was similar to the more popular Bull Terrier, 15 to 18 inches. Breeders were producing Staffordshires that were too heavy and not mobile, so by 1948 the height diminished to 14 to 16

The English Bull Terrier, distinguished by its unique head shape, is a taller, heavier dog than the Staffordshire. Both breeds derived from bull and terrier crosses.

inches. This change was not welcome by many breeders and dogs today still push the height requirement of the standard. In modern times, breeders have concerned themselves with achieving the perfect head on their Staffordshire Bull Terriers. It is fair to say that the heads of the breed have received too much emphasis and the hindquarters and shoulders have suffered, resulting in movement that is far from ideal in most dogs.

THE UNITED STATES

Many British industrial and mine workers opted to immigrate to the United States in the 1860s and 1870s. These hardworking Britons brought their Staffordshire Bull Terriers with them and resumed breeding them in the States, often

A champion-quality Staffordshire Bull Terrier by the name of Ruff-n-Tuff, stands 16.5 inches and 40 pounds.

with other terrier types. These dogs became known as Yankee Terriers, American Bull Terriers and American (Pit) Bull Terriers (as if placing parentheses around the 'pit' would soften the blow). These dogs were admired by the American public and revered for their devotion to family and children. Although not the size of most guard dogs, these dogs compared in courage and determination.

These dogs were also used in dog fights, as were many similar dogs that arrived with Irish immigrants. The United Kennel Club (UKC) was established as a registry for these pit bull dogs, which were refused acceptance by the larger American

Kennel Club (AKC). The prestigious, and somewhat pigheaded, AKC did not grant the American Pit Bull Terrier recognition, though it would later recognise the same dog by the name of the Staffordshire Terrier in 1936. The first Staffordshire Terrier registered with AKC was Wheeler's Black Dinah. Many fanciers took advantage of the situation and dual-registered their dogs as Staffordshire Terriers with the AKC and as American (Pit) Bull Terriers with the UKC. (To further confuse matters, the American Dog Breeders Association, a national association for dogmen of the pit variety, registered the breed as the Staffordshire Terrier in the late 1930s.)

The parent club, the Staffordshire Terrier Club of America, was formed on May 23, 1936 to protect 'The Grand Old Breed' formerly known as the American (Pit) Bull Terrier or Yankee Terrier. The standard

American Staffordshire Terrier is the name that the American Kennel Club adopted in the U.S. when the Staffordshire Terrier breed split. This is a handsome American Staffordshire.

was drawn up straight away and Staffordshire Terriers entered the show rings. The first American shows were held in conjunction with the International Kennel Club of Chicago in the late 1930s and as many as 50 dogs were exhibited. The first AKC champion of record was Maher's Captain D who garnered the title in 1937. Arguably the most famous Staffordshire Terrier of this early period was Champion X-Pert Brindle Biff, owned and bred by Clifford A. Ormsby.

As the gap of type variation expanded to a grand canyon within the breed, breeders decided to split the Staffordshire Terrier into two breeds. In 1972 the American Staffordshire Terrier was recognised, and two years later, the Staffordshire Bull Terrier reappeared on the scene. Employing the same name used by Joe Dunn in England in the 1930s, the Staffordshire Bull Terrier is the

A young white Staffordshire Bull Terrier. Although not as commonly seen, solid white is an allowable colour according to The Kennel Club standard.

shorter legged, thicker dog, weighing 24 to 38 pounds (11 to 17 kgs) and standing 14 to 16 inches (35.5 to 40.5 cms). The American Staffordshire Terrier stands on taller legs and is 17 to 19 inches in height (42.5 to 48 cms). Of course, the Staffordshire Bull Terrier in America still resembled the conformation of the original British dogs. Since the type of dog that became known as the American Staffordshire Terrier had no following in England, there was no similar controversy or dissension among fanciers. Although recognised as two distinct breeds (three, if you're inclined to include the UKC's American Pit Bull Terrier), these dogs are genetically similar, though the lines haven't been crossed in many generations.

This Staffordshire Bull Terrier possesses an impressive expansive chest and the desired musculature that is characteristic of the breed.

21

Some Staffordshire Bull Terrier owners are very passionate about their dogs. What more appropriate tribute to a Staffordshire than to tattoo its image on your arm!

PERSONALITY AND CHARACTERISTICS OF THE
Staffordshire Bull Terrier

For all the blood-curdling history of the Staffordshire, many astounding positive qualities permeate through every pore of the breed. The Staffordshire Bull Terrier is defined not only by its 'indomitable courage and tenacity' but also by its unflinching affection for children. At first glance, such qualities appear contradictory. How could a formidable, fearless fighter be expected to curl up with the children at sundown? Who could expect that a dog bred to kill other dogs would be the choice of thousands of dog lovers around the world and be trusted with their children?

To understand this contradiction, the reader must identify which qualities in the Staffordshire Bull Terrier inspired the animal to undertake the Battle Royal, the fight to the death with a fellow canine. The quality is pure and simple: absolute devotion to mankind. No breed on earth desires to please its human owner more than the Staffordshire! The tenacity and courage of the breed are equally matched by its love of humans and its desire to please them. Staffordshires also recognise the tenderness and frailty of children, which inspires their dedication to and protection of them.

Historically, the Staffordshire Bull Terrier has earned the pet names 'The Children's Nursemaid' or 'The Nanny Dog,' celebrating the breed's fondness of children. Owners must also understand that children should never be left unsupervised with any dog, regardless of its size or temperament. Given the breed's stoic nature and resistance to pain, the Staffordshire can tolerate childhandling. Nevertheless, children must be properly instructed to handle a dog. Children's natural exuberance can sometimes promote mistreating a dog.

Staffordshire Bull Terriers are devoted, loyal and caring as companions. They usually get along famously with children.

The original 'Nanny Dog,' the Staffordshire is a fun-loving dog that makes a loving, protective pet for most children.

Another quality endears the Staffordshire to children: its love of fun. The Staffordshire is an active, athletic and oftimes silly dog. Its comical antics and games of chase and fetch delight the likes of children and adults. There is no doubt about the athletic abilities of a Staffordshire. Just a mere glance at the dog's musculature, from head to toe, reveals that this is an active person's choice. The cheeks are prominently muscled, giving the dog incredible holding strength with its jaws. Many owners provide their dogs swinging ropes and even tyres for exercise. The dog's feet are well padded and strong, connected to an athlete's muscular legs. Ever see a Staffordshire in mid-air? What amazing strength and balance this little terrier possesses! When a Staffordshire flexes, whether he's pouncing vertically upward or just smiling, it's a joy to behold!

The Staffordshire Bull Terrier puts his muscle where his pearly whites are: this is an unstoppable watchdog for family and property. For his pounds, the Staffordshire ranks first amongst the guard dogs, as he is the smallest of the capable canine defenders. Whilst many of his relatives, the Mastiff, Bullmastiff, and Boxer, stand many inches taller than the Staffordshire, the breed compensates with its solid strength and unshakeable devotion to those it is protecting. A bullet doesn't need to be large to be effective: the Staffordshire, perfectly aimed and propelled,

Staffordshire puppies are fun dogs with a true sense of comic timing. They give as much pleasure to the spectator as to their playmates.

A tyre swing makes a marvelous form of entertainment for the Staffordshire. This athletic bloke is showing off his persistence and the superior strength of his jaw.

25

Staffordshire Bull Terriers are wonderful retrievers and truly enjoy sharing time with their owners. The Staffordshire is game for any game you can conjure up.

can stop a would-be perpetrator in his tracks. Tenacity and strength are intermingled to make this dog fearless and formidable. Keep in mind, however, that the Staffordshire is not a true guard dog; unlike the Dobermann and Bullmastiff, the breed was not designed as a protector.

Is every Staffordshire friendly, trustworthy, and even-tempered? Breeders will contend that most Staffordshires do possess these qualities in spades, though not all. Friendliness should indeed define the breed, though most breeds and most dogs should be friendly. Most breed standards include the word 'friendly' in the description of

A highly recommended way to send Christmas greetings! Here's Wildstaff Nightmare masquerading as an elfin wonder.

the breed's characteristics. The Kennel Club breed standard also includes the words 'totally reliable,' assuring the reader that the Staffordshire Bull Terrier is beyond trustworthy in the ideal circumstances. Provided that the dog has been properly reared and socialised, there should be no question regarding the friendliness and reliability of the dog. Obviously dogs that are not treated kindly, trained and raised with intelligence and responsibility cannot be as consistently dependable.

The evenness of the Staffordshire's temperament stems in part from the breed's history in the dog pit. Dog fighters raised and bred dogs to be totally predictable. These are powerful, tenacious, aggressive dogs that must be 'totally reliable.' As disturbing as the image may be, the owner of the losing Staffordshire in a dog fight had to trust his dog enough, even when the dog was mangled and in pain, to pick him up and treat his wounds. These dogs, often in shock as well as horrific pain, never attempted to bite at their masters' hand. Such dogs were strictly dog-aggressive, never people-aggressive, even in dire, unfathomable circumstances.

That's why your four-year-old can step on your Staffordshire's toes without the dog reacting defensively. That's why the family cat can swat at your Staffordshire's tail and get no reaction except a yawn. A dog that would sacrifice his well being, in fact his life, for his owner's satisfaction is a dog that could be relied upon in any situation.

Staffordshires are adaptable but sensitive. You cannot mistreat a Staffordshire. These dogs should not be harshly reprimanded nor unfairly dismissed. They live to please their owner, and nothing is as crushing to a Staffordshire as his owner's anger or displeasure.

While firmness and fairness should define your treatment of a Staffordshire, the dog must always sense that you are pleased with his actions. Praise to a Staffordshire is nothing short of glorious.

Staffordshires can adapt to practically any situation and handle whatever tasks and challenges are set before them, provided the owner treats the dog properly. Many Staffordshires have made happy 'relocations' from country life to the big city. Provided they receive proper exercise, they can live comfortably in a small flat, though they are most content with plenty of room to run and play. City dwellers frequently visit the parks to allow their dogs the opportunity to run, though a

Staffordshire Bull Terriers can thrive in the big city as long as they are taken on frequent walks. Meeting friends in the park is a plus to city life.

27

Staffordshire Bull Terrier does not suffer from susceptibility to many congenital illnesses, though bilateral cataracts and kidney stones are reported, as are harelips and cleft palates in newborns. Cystine uroliths affect the kidneys and bladder of Staffordshires. These stones, formed by crystals, cause the disease known as urolithiasis. Vets usually prescribe antibiotics to treat these infections.

A dog that develops a cataract will have cloudiness in the eye that can lead to blindness. Although surgery can help, the dog's sight cannot be restored to that of a normal dog. Annual checkups will help detect cataracts, and an affected dog should not be bred. Bilateral cataracts, also known as juvenile cataracts, occur in younger dogs, and are hereditary in the Staffordshire. The most commonly identified cataract is found in the posterior axial subcapsular region of the lens. Such cataracts mature as the dog grows older. In certain cases, the cataract can be detected in one eye before the other eye appears affected. In severe cases, the dog can go blind because of the intensity of the opacities.

Breeders and vets warn new Staffordshire owners to watch

leash is always necessary whenever your Staffordshire will be meeting strange dogs and people.

The Staffordshire's sensitivity can only be present in a dog of extreme intelligence. Staffordshires tend to be adept problem-solvers, possessing powers that border on reasoning. They are tenacious and patient, rarely tiring over a challenge.

The Staffordshire Bull Terrier is amongst the healthiest of purebred dogs.

HEALTH CONSIDERATIONS OF THE STAFFORDSHIRE
Unlike many breeds of purebred dogs, the Staffordshire is highly resistant to sickness. The

their dogs carefully. The breed has a very high pain threshold and can adjust to great discomfort without the owner realising a problem. Staffordshires commonly succumb to joint and limb injuries, which can go unnoticed in many dogs.

Staffordshire Bull Terriers presently enjoy strong resistance to most orthopaedic diseases, although there is concern in the breed about hip dysplasia. Compared to other popular breeds, the Staffordshire's incidence of hip dysplasia is quite minimal. Breeders recommend screening their stock

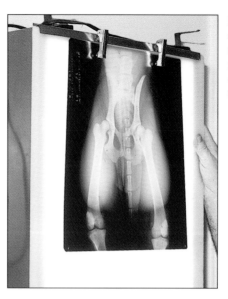

Hip dysplasia can only be confirmed by a radiologist's evaluation of an x-ray.

animals before including them in a breeding programme. It's estimated that about one percent of the Staffordshire population suffers from severe hip dysplasia, while about 20 percent test for some degree of dysplasia. In this 20 percent, most dogs will experience little if any discomfort, though it varies from dog to dog. Since hip dysplasia is a congenital illness, none of these dogs should be bred to keep the population dysplasia-free. Other orthopaedic concerns, even less serious than hip dysplasia, are elbow dysplasia and patellar luxation (affecting the kneecaps). Both the knees and the elbows can be screened for problems, but this has not yet become as commonplace as x-raying for faulty hips.

Staffordshire Bull Terriers prize the company of their owners. An excellent choice for women who live alone, Staffordshire are devoted and determined protectors.

29

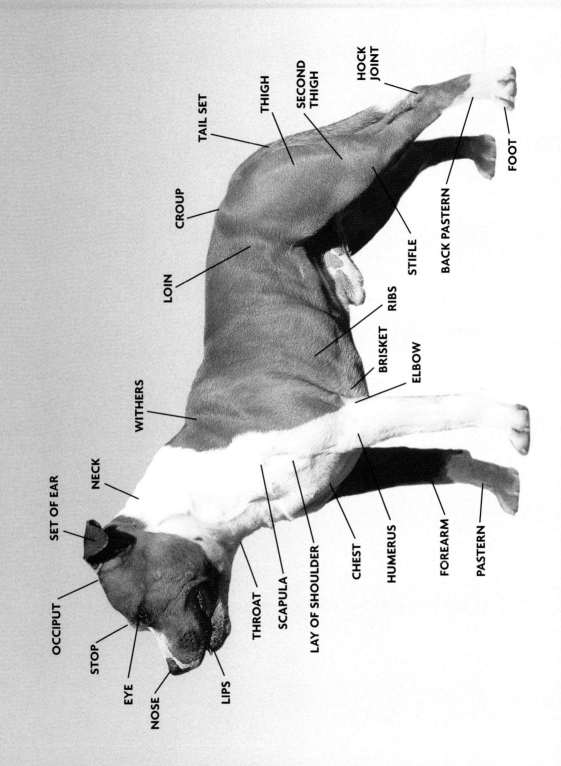

OCCIPUT

SET OF EAR

STOP

EYE

NOSE

LIPS

THROAT

SCAPULA

LAY OF SHOULDER

CHEST

HUMERUS

FOREARM

PASTERN

NECK

WITHERS

LOIN

CROUP

TAIL SET

THIGH

SECOND THIGH

HOCK JOINT

STIFLE

BACK PASTERN

FOOT

BRISKET

RIBS

ELBOW

THE BREED STANDARD FOR THE
Staffordshire Bull Terrier

WHAT IS A STANDARD?

A breed standard is the official description of the way a dog should look and act. The standard is drafted by the parent club and then adopted by The Kennel Club, the national registering body for purebred dogs. It is the accepted 'bible' for breeders and judges to evaluate the quality of Staffordshire Bull Terriers. Dogs shown in exhibition are compared to the breed standard. Only those dogs that 'stack up' to the standard will earn the title of champion and therefore be deemed worthy of breeding.

While the standard is subject to the interpretation of the judge and breeder, it does attempt to emphasise the most important aspects of the dog. The Staffordshire Bull Terrier is first and foremost a strong, solid dog. The standard refers to its musculature five times, as well as two other references to its · strength.

Depending on the nation that you're visiting, the standard may vary from place to place. Throughout the United Kingdom, The Kennel Club standard is the accepted standard. Throughout the European Union nations, the standard of the Fédération Cynologique Internationale is the accepted standard.

THE KENNEL CLUB STANDARD FOR THE STAFFORDSHIRE BULL TERRIER

General Appearance: Smooth-coated, well balanced, of great strength for his size. Muscular, active and agile.

Characteristics: Traditionally of indomitable courage and tenacity. Highly intelligent and affectionate especially with children.

Staffordshire Bull Terriers should appear muscular, active and agile, even when standing at attention.

Rose or half pricked-ears that are balanced with the head are preferred in the Staffordshire Bull Terrier.

Temperament: Bold, fearless and totally reliable.

Head and Skull: Short, deep though with broad skull. Very pronounced cheek muscles, distinct stop, short foreface, nose black.

Eyes: Dark preferred but may bear some relation to coat colour. Round, of medium size, and set to look straight ahead. Eye rims dark.

Ears: Rose or half-pricked, not large or heavy. Full, drop or pricked ears highly undesirable.

The teeth must be large with a perfect scissors bite.

Mouth: Lips tight and clean. Jaws strong, teeth large, with a perfect, regular and complete scissors bite, i.e., upper teeth closely overlapping lower teeth and set square to the jaws.

Neck: Muscular, rather short, clean in outline gradually widening towards shoulders.

Forequarters: Legs straight and well boned, set rather wide apart, showing no weakness at the pasterns, from which point feet turn out a little. Shoulders well laid back with no looseness at elbow.

Body: Close-coupled, with level topline, wide front, deep brisket, well sprung ribs; muscular and well defined.

Hindquarters: Well muscled, hocks well let down with stifles well bent. Legs parallel when viewed from behind.

Feet: Well padded, strong and of medium size. Nails black in solid coloured dogs.

Tail: Medium length, low-set, tapering to a point and carried rather low. Should not curl much and may be likened to an old-fashioned pump handle.

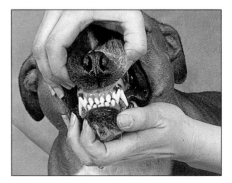

Gait/Movement: Free, powerful and agile with economy of effort. Legs moving parallel when viewed from front or rear. Discernible drive from hindlegs.

Coat: Smooth, short and close.

Colour: Red, fawn, white, black or blue, or any one of these colours with white. Any shade of brindle or any shade of brindle with white. Black and tan or liver colour highly undesirable.

Size: Desirable height at withers 35.5. to 40 cms (14 to 16 ins),

The Staffordshire's body should be close coupled with a level topline.

The white blaze on the Staffordshire's chest is characteristic of the breed. The blaze gives the impression of an even broader chest.

these heights being related to the weights. Weight: dogs: 12.7 to 17 kgs (28 to 38 lbs); bitches 11 to 15.4 kgs (24 to 34 lbs).

Faults: Any departure from the foregoing points should be considered a fault and the seriousness with which the fault should be regarded should be in exact proportion to its degree.

Note: Male animals should have two apparently normal testicles fully descended into the scrotum.

The red colouration is a very popular and attractive choice in Staffordshires. Judges do not place great importance on colouration, provided the dogs are not liver or black and tan.

33

	CORRECT	**INCORRECT**

EARS

Rose ears that are too large and pricked ears (appearing almost cropped) are undesirable in the Staffordshire.

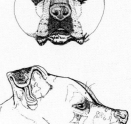

FOREFACE

The stop should be distinct and the foreface short. Lack of stop ruins the expression of the Staffordshire.

FOREQUARTERS

The legs should be straight and well boned, never loose, bending in or out, at the elbows. The chest should be broad.

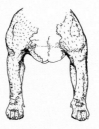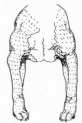

HINDQUARTERS

The hindlegs should be parallel when viewed from behind, never bowing in at the hocks.

TAIL

The desired tail is likened to an old-fashioned pump handle, never curling or carried high.

Staffordshire Bull Terrier

ARE YOU READY FOR THE STAFFORDSHIRE?

The Staffordshire Bull Terrier offers the potential owner many advantages. This is a very easy-care dog; obedient, smooth-coated, intelligent and remarkably healthy. For an active dog owner who is willing to spend quality time with a dog, the Staffordshire is an excellent choice. The breed's dedication to home and family, its protective nature and its good-hearted spirit make the Staffordshire a king amongst canines.

DID YOU KNOW?

If you lead an erratic, unpredictable life, with daily or weekly changes in your work requirements, consider the problems of owning a puppy. The new puppy has to be fed regularly, socialised (loved, petted, handled, introduced to other people) and, most importantly, allowed to visit outdoors for toilet training. As the dog gets older, it can be more tolerant of deviations in its feeding and toilet relief.

In the hands of a responsible owner, the Staffordshire has few flaws.

The question remains, are you that responsible owner? Make no mistake: you will be the beginning, middle and end of

The Staffordshire Bull Terrier is protective and devoted, making an alert guard dog for family and home.

your Staffordshire's world. This is not a dog you can ignore. You will be his favourite friend, walking companion, snoozing lap and dinner chum. Are you ready to 'own' an unconditional best friend whom you raise from the tender age of eight weeks? Staffordshires abound in energy, more so than the average dog. They seek companionship and entertainment, and they love to entertain! An active, if not athletic, individual is the best owner for a Staffordshire. Your Staffordshire will enjoy an afternoon cycling or jogging on the beach, running aside you on horseback or playing chase in the garden. These kinds of activities keep the Staffordshire healthy in mind and body.

DID YOU KNOW?

You should not even think about buying a puppy that looks sick, undernourished, overly frightened or nervous. Sometimes a timid puppy will warm up to you after a 30-minute 'let's-get-acquainted' session.

Selecting a Staff puppy is not a simple task. Choose a puppy that is well socialised—never shy, nervous or aggressive.

WHERE TO BEGIN?

If you are convinced that the Staffordshire Bull Terrier is the ideal dog for you, it's time to find where to find a puppy and what to look for. Locating a litter of Staffordshires should not present a problem for the new owner. You should inquire about breeders in your area who enjoy a good reputation in the breed. You are looking for an established breeder with outstanding dog ethics and a strong commitment to the breed. New owners should have as many questions as they have doubts. An established breeder is indeed the one to answer your four million questions and make you comfort-

able with your choice of the Staffordshire Bull Terrier. An established breeder will sell you a puppy at a fair price if, and only if, the breeder determines that you are a suitable, worthy owner of his/her dogs. An established breeder can be relied upon for advice, no matter what time of day or night. A reputable breeder will accept a puppy back, without questions, should you decide that this not the right dog for you.

When choosing a breeder, reputation is much more important than a convenient location. Owning a dog is not really a convenience, so convenience doesn't play a part, like responsibility and commit-ment do. It's not convenient to have a four-legged wolf creature crawling around your house, chewing, piddling and messing every room it enters. We don't choose to share our homes with dogs because it's convenient, but rather for the other fringe benefits to this thing we call dog ownership. The local novice breeder, trying so hard to get rid of that first litter of ten puppies, is more than accommodating and anxious to sell you one. That breeder lives only a couple of miles away but will charge you as much as any established breeder. The novice breeder isn't going to interrogate you and your family about your intentions with the puppy, the environment and training you can provide, etc. That breeder will be nowhere to be found when your poorly bred, badly adjusted four-pawed monster starts to growl and spit up at midnight or eat the family cat!

While health consid-

While colour should not be a major factor is selecting a puppy, signs of good health and sound temperament must play key roles in your choice.

erations in the Staffordshire are not nearly as daunting as in most other breeds, socialisation is a breeder concern of immense importance. Since the Staffordshire has a natural aggressive nature towards other dogs, socialisation is the first and best way to prevent this instinct from developing into a problem. Good breeders introduce their puppies to other dogs at an early age to promote their acceptance of fellow canines.

DID YOU KNOW?

Your selection of a good puppy can be determined by your needs. A show potential or a good pet? It is your choice. Every puppy, however, should be of good temperament. Although show-quality puppies are bred and raised with emphasis on physical conformation, responsible breeders strive for equally good temperament. Do not buy from a breeder who concentrates solely on physical beauty at the expense of personality.

CHOOSING A BREEDER

Choosing a breeder is an important first step in dog ownership. Fortunately, the majority of Staffordshire breeders are devoted to the breed and its well being. New owners should have little problem finding a reputable breeder who doesn't live on the other side of the country (or in a different country). The Kennel Club is able to recommend breeders of quality

37

DID YOU KNOW?
If the breeder from whom you are buying a puppy asks you a lot of personal questions, do not be insulted. Such a breeder wants to be sure that you will be a fit provider for his puppy.

Choose a pup with a sweet personality that wants to get close to you. A well-socialised Staffordshire puppy thrives on the company of humans.

Staffordshires, as can any local all-breed club or Staffordshire club. Potential owners are encouraged to attend a dog show to see the Staffordshires in action, to meet the breeders and handlers firsthand, and to get an idea what Staffordshires look like outside of a photographer's lens. Provided you approach the handlers when they are not engaged in grooming or handling the dogs, most are more than willing to answer questions, recommend breeders and give advice.

Now that you have contacted and met a breeder or two and made your choice about which breeder is best suited to your needs, it's time to visit the litter. Keep in mind that many top breeders have waiting lists. Sometimes new owners have to wait as long as two years for a puppy. If you are really committed to the breeder whom you've

selected, then you will wait (and hope for an early arrival!). If not, you may have to resort to your second or third choice breeder. Don't be too anxious, however. If the breeder doesn't have any waiting list, or any customers, there is probably a good reason. It's no different than visiting a pub with no clientele. The better pubs and restaurants always have a waiting list—and it's usually worth the wait. Besides, isn't a puppy more important than a pint?

Staffordshire puppies can be feisty and a bit quarrelsome, but

the new owner should never select the puppy who appears to be a mean-spirited instigator. A sweet-natured puppy with an outgoing personality is the new owner's best choice. When viewing a litter of Staffordshire puppies, you are looking for friendly, bright-eyed pups. Hopefully that describes the whole litter, although there is usually one shy pup who cannot compete with the rest. Breeders commonly allow visitors to see the litter by around the fifth or sixth week, and puppies leave for their new homes between the eighth and tenth week. Breeders who permit their puppies to leave early are more interested in your pounds than their puppies' well being. Puppies need to learn the rules of the trade from their

Since the Staffordshire's most vital component is its love of people, new owners must seek puppies that are friendly, personable and comfortable in the arms of a stranger.

DID YOU KNOW?

Breeders rarely release puppies until they are at least eight weeks of age. This is an acceptable age for most breeds of dog, excepting toy breeds which are not released until around 12 weeks, given their petite sizes. If a breeder has a puppy that is 12 weeks or more, it is hopefully well socialised and housetrained. Be sure that it is otherwise healthy before deciding to take it home.

dams, and most dams continue teaching the pups manners, and dos and don'ts until around the eighth week. Breeders spend significant amounts of time with the Staffordshire toddlers so that they are able to interact with the 'other species,' i.e., humans! Staffordshires get on well with humans but other canines concern them. Given the long history that dogs and humans have, bonding between the two species is natural but must be nurtured. A well-bred, well-socialised Staffordshire

39

pup wants nothing more than to be near you and please you. That's as convenient as a puppy can be!

What other considerations might an owner entertain in choosing a pup? Most breeders agree that the sex of the puppy is

'You can't teach an old dog new tricks' is an untrue expression, but it is easier to train a pup.

immaterial. Staffordshires usually cannot cohabitate in same sex pairs, so owners considering a pair must get a male and a female.

Colouration is probably the most common preference amongst new owners. Certainly some handsome Staffordshire in this book has caught the reader's eye and convinced him of one colour over another. Breeders do not place much importance on colour, although liver and black and tan are strictly prohibited from the show ring. This seemingly random prejudice stems from interbreeding of the Staffordshire with some liver and black and tan breeds in the past. Today such crosses are frowned upon. Regardless of which colour the new owner favours, dark pigment on the nose and paw pads is important. The temperament and structure of the puppy must be considered before colour. As long as the puppy is outgoing and

An athlete at heart, the Staffordshire has strong legs to match his strong jaws. An active person with time to exercise the dog is the best owner for the Staff.

friendly and has a compact and cobby body with a strong head, well in balance with the body, you will have an ideal Staffordshire Bull Terrier.

COMMITMENT OF OWNERSHIP
After considering all of these factors, you have most likely already made some very important decisions about selecting your puppy. You have chosen a Staffordshire, which means that you have decided which characteristics you want in a dog and what type of dog will best fit into your family and lifestyle. If you

have selected a breeder, you have gone a step further—you have done your research and found a responsible, conscientious person who breeds quality Staffordshires and who should be a reliable source of help as you and your puppy adjust to life together. If you have observed a litter in action, you have obtained a firsthand look at the dynamics of a puppy 'pack' and, thus, you have gotten to learn about each pup's individual personality—perhaps you have even found one that particularly appeals to you.

However, even if you have not yet found the Staffordshire puppy of your dreams, observing pups will help you learn to recognise certain behaviour and to determine what a pup's behaviour indicates about his temperament. You will be able to pick out which pups are the leaders, which ones are less outgoing, which ones are confident, which ones are shy, playful, friendly, aggressive, etc. Equally as important, you will learn to recognise what a healthy pup should look and act like. All of these things will help you in your search,

When you buy a Staff puppy, you are entering into a 15-year commitment. Don't make the decision to own a Staff too hastily.

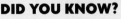

DID YOU KNOW?

Taking your dog from the breeder to your home in a car can be a very uncomfortable experience for both of you. The puppy will have been taken from his warm, friendly, safe environment and brought into a strange new environment. An environment that moves. Be prepared for loose bowels, urination, crying, whining and even fear biting. With proper love and encouragement when you arrive home, the stress of the trip should quickly disappear.

and when you find the Staffordshire that was meant for you, you will know it!

Researching your breed, selecting a responsible breeder and observing as many pups as possible are all important steps on the way to dog ownership. It may seem like a lot of effort…and you have not even brought the pup home yet! Remember, though, you cannot be too careful when it comes to deciding on the type of dog you want and finding out about your prospective pup's background. Buying a puppy is not—or should not be—just another whimsical purchase. This is one instance in which you actually do get to choose your own family! You may be thinking that buying a puppy should be fun—it should not be so serious

41

Children should be instructed to properly handle puppies. Parents must take the responsibility of tempering the child's natural excitement around puppies.

and so much work. Keep in mind that your puppy is not a cuddly stuffed toy or decorative lawn ornament, but a creature who will become a real member of your family, and you will realise that while buying a puppy is a pleasurable and exciting endeavour, it is not something to be taken lightly. Relax…the fun will start when the pup comes home!

Always keep in mind that a puppy is nothing more than a baby in a furry disguise…a baby who is virtually helpless in a human world and who trusts his

Kissing your Staffordshire, or any dog, on the mouth is quite unsanitary.

owner for fulfilment of his basic needs for survival. In addition to water and shelter, your pup needs care, protection, guidance and love. If you are not prepared to commit to this, then you are not prepared to own a dog.

Wait a minute, you say. How hard could this be? All of my neighbours own dogs and they seem to be doing just fine. Why should I have to worry about all of this? Well, you should not worry about it; in fact, you will probably find that once your Staffordshire pup gets used to his new home, he will fall into his place in the family quite natural-

ly. But it never hurts to emphasize the commitment of dog ownership. With some time and patience, it is really not too difficult to raise a curious and exuberant Staffordshire pup to be a well-adjusted and well-mannered adult dog—a dog that could be your most loyal friend.

DID YOU KNOW?
It will take at least two weeks for your puppy to become accustomed to his new surroundings. Give him lots of love, attention, handling, frequent opportunities to relieve himself, a diet he is used to and a place he can call his own.

PREPARING PUPPY'S PLACE IN YOUR HOME

Researching your breed and finding a breeder are only two aspects of the 'homework' you will have to do before bringing your Staffordshire puppy home. You will also have to prepare your home and family for the new addition. Much like you would prepare a nursery for a newborn baby, you will need to designate a place in your home that will be the puppy's own. How you prepare your home will depend on how much freedom the dog will be allowed. Will he be

confined to one room or a specific area in the house, or will he be allowed to roam as he pleases? Will he spend most of his time in the house or will he be primarily an outdoor dog? Whatever you decide, you must ensure that he has a place that he can 'call his own.'

When you bring your new puppy into your home, you are bringing him into what will become his home as well. Obviously, you did not buy a puppy so that he could take over your house, but in order for a puppy to grow into a stable, well-adjusted dog, he has to feel comfortable in his surroundings. Remember, he is leaving the warmth and security of his mother and littermates, as well as the familiarity of the only place he has ever known, so it is important to make his transition

These Staff puppies are enjoying a photo opportunity in a strange environment.

Breeders often allow children into the whelping area to meet their puppies. Giving the puppies as much exposure to different experiences is key to the social-isation process.

43

as easy as possible. By preparing a place in your home for the puppy, you are making him feel as welcome as possible in a strange new place. It should not take him long to get used to it, but the sudden shock of being transplanted is somewhat traumatic for a young pup. Imagine how a small child would feel in the same situation—that is how your puppy must be feeling. It is up to you to reassure him and to let him know, 'Little fellow, you are going to like it here!'

WHAT YOU SHOULD BUY
CRATE

To someone unfamiliar with the use of crates in dog training, it may seem like punishment to shut a dog in a crate. However, this is not the case at all. Crates are not cruel—crates have many humane and highly effective uses in dog care and training. For example, crate training is a very popular and very successful housebreaking method. A crate can keep your dog safe during travel; and, perhaps most importantly, a crate provides your dog with a place of

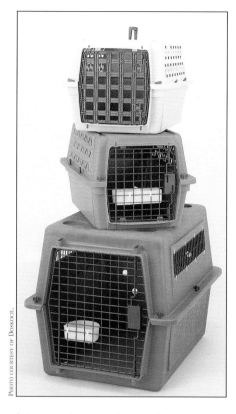

PHOTO COURTESY OF DOSKOCIL.

his own in your home. It serves as a 'doggie bedroom' of sorts—your Staffordshire can curl up in his crate when he wants to sleep or when he just needs a break. Many dogs sleep in their crates overnight. When lined with soft blankets and his favourite toy, a crate becomes a cosy pseudo-den for your dog. Like his ancestors, he too will seek out the comfort and retreat of a den—you just happen to be providing him with something a little more luxurious than leaves and twigs lining a dirty ditch.

As far as purchasing a crate, the type that you buy is up to you. It will most likely be one of the two most popular types: wire or fibreglass. There are advantages and disadvantages to each type. For example, a wire crate is more open, allowing the air to flow through and affording the dog a view of what is going on around him. A fibreglass crate, however, is sturdier and can double as a travel crate since it provides more protection for the dog. The size of the crate is another thing to consider. Puppies do not stay puppies forever—in fact, sometimes it seems as if they grow right before your eyes. A Yorkie-sized crate may be fine for a very young Staffordshire pup, but it will not do him much good for long! Unless you have the money and the inclination to buy a new crate every time your pup

has a growth spurt, it is better to get one that will accommodate your dog both as a pup and at full size. A medium-size crate will be necessary for a full-grown Staffordshire, as their approximate weight range is between 28 and 34 pounds.

BEDDING
A blanket or two in the dog's crate will help the dog feel more at home. First, the blankets will take the place of the leaves, twigs, etc., that the pup would use in the wild to make a den; the pup can make his own 'burrow' in the

The most valuable accessory you can buy for your Staff is a crate. It will become invaluable in training. It is really a doggie bedroom.

DID YOU KNOW?
During crate training, you should partition off the section of the crate in which the pup stays. If he is given too big of an area, this will hinder your training efforts. Crate training is based on the fact that a dog does not like to soil his sleeping quarters, so it is ineffective to keep a pup in a crate that is so big that he can eliminate in one end and get far enough away from it to sleep. Also, you want to make the crate den-like for the pup. Blankets and a favourite toy will make the crate cosy for the small Staffordshire; as he grows, you may want to evict some of his 'roommates' to make more room.

It will take some coaxing at first, but be patient. Given some time to get used to it, your pup will adapt to his new home-within-a-home quite nicely.

45

crate. Although your pup is far removed from his den-making ancestors, the denning instinct is still a part of his genetic makeup. Second, until you bring your pup home, he has been sleeping amidst the warmth of his mother and littermates, and while a blanket is not the same as a warm, breathing body, it still provides heat and something with which to snuggle. You will want to wash your pup's blankets frequently in case he has an accident in his crate, and replace or remove any blanket that becomes ragged and starts to fall apart.

Toys

Toys are a must for dogs of all ages, especially for curious playful pups. Puppies are the 'children' of the dog world, and what child does not love toys? Chew toys provide enjoyment to both dog and owner—your dog will enjoy playing with his favourite toys, while you will enjoy the fact that they distract

DID YOU KNOW?
With a big variety of dog toys available, and so many that look like they would be a lot of fun for a dog, be careful in your selection. It is amazing what a set of puppy teeth can do to an innocent-looking toy, so, obviously, safety is a major consideration. Be sure to choose the most durable products that you can find. Hard nylon bones and toys are a safe bet, and many of them are offered in different scents and flavours that will be sure to capture your Staffordshire's attention. It is always fun to play a game of catch with your dog, and there are balls and flying discs that are specially made to withstand dog teeth.

him from your expensive shoes and leather sofa. Puppies love to chew; in fact, chewing is a physical need for pups as they are teething, and everything looks appetizing! The full range of your possessions—from old dishrag to Oriental rug—are fair game in the eyes of a teething pup. Puppies are not all that discerning when it comes to finding something to literally 'sink their teeth into'— everything tastes great!

Staffordshire puppies are fairly aggressive chewers and only

A tyre swing may seem unconventional as a dog toy, but it is a great exercise device for the Staff. It is one of the few toys through which they cannot readily chew.

Your local pet shop should have a variety of toys made especially for dogs. Never give human toys to your Staff.

PHOTO COURTESY OF MIKKI PET PRODUCTS.

DID YOU KNOW?

The majority of problems that are commonly seen in young pups will disappear as your Staffordshire gets older. However, how you deal with problems when he is young will determine how he reacts to discipline as an adult dog. It is important to establish who is boss (hopefully it will be you!) right away when you are first bonding with your Staffordshire. This bond will set the tone for the rest of your life together.

the hardest, strongest toys should be offered to them. Breeders advise owners to resist stuffed toys, because they can become de-stuffed in no time. The overly excited pup may ingest the stuffing, which is neither digestible nor nutritious.

Similarly, squeaky toys are quite popular, but must be avoided for the Staffordshire. Perhaps a squeaky toy can be used as an aid in training, but not for free play. If a pup 'disembowels' one of these, the small plastic squeaker inside can be dangerous if swallowed. Monitor the condition of all your pup's toys

47

The Staffordshire's strength is evident just by looking at him! Therefore, it is important to purchase only leads and collars made of the most durable materials for your Staff.

carefully and get rid of any that have been chewed to the point of becoming potentially dangerous.

Be careful of natural bones, which have a tendency to splinter into sharp, dangerous pieces. Also be careful of rawhide, which can turn into pieces that are easy to swallow or into a mushy mess on your carpet.

Many collars suitable for Staffs have metal beads imbedded in them. These beads are attractive and discourage chewing should collar become accessible to the dog's mouth.

LEAD
A nylon lead is probably the best option as it is the most resistant to puppy teeth should your pup take a liking to chewing on his lead. Of course, this is a habit that should be nipped in the bud, but if your pup likes to chew on his lead he has a very slim chance of being able to chew through the strong nylon. Nylon leads are also lightweight, which is good for a young Staffordshire who is just getting used to the idea of walking on a lead. For everyday walking and safety purposes, the nylon

lead is a good choice. As your pup grows up and gets used to walking on the lead, and can do it politely, you may want to purchase a flexible lead, which allows you to extend the length to give the dog a broader area to explore or to pull in the lead when you want to keep him close. Of course there are special leads for training purposes, and specially made leather harnesses for the working Staffordshires, but these are not necessary for routine walks As your Staffordshire grows into his muscles, you may want to purchase something stronger, like a thicker leather lead.

COLLAR
Your pup should get used to wearing a collar all the time since you will want to attach his ID tags to it. Also, you have to attach the

the collar. It may take some time
for your pup to get used to
wearing the collar, but soon he
will not even notice that it is
there. Choke collars are to be used
for training, but only by an owner
who knows exactly how to use it.
When you change to a stronger
leather or a chain lead to walk
your Staffordshire, you will need
a stronger collar as well.

Since Staff
puppies can
easily chew
through cheap
plastic bowls,
only high quality
bowls should be
considered.
Stainless steel
bowls are the
best choice.

Accustom the
puppy to the
collar at a young
age. Buckle
collars are
acceptable for
young puppies.
Identification
tags can be
attached to the
buckle collar.

lead to something! A lightweight
nylon collar is a good choice;
make sure that it fits snugly
enough so that the pup cannot
wriggle out of it, but is loose
enough so that it will not be
uncomfortably tight around the
pup's neck. You should be able to
fit a finger between the pup and

Photo Courtesy of Mikki Pet Products.

FOOD AND WATER BOWLS

Your pup will need two bowls, one for food and one for water. You may want two sets of bowls, one for inside and one for outside, depending on where the dog will be fed and where he will be spending most of his time. Stainless steel or sturdy plastic bowls are popular choices. Plastic bowls are more chewable. Dogs tend not to chew on the steel variety, which can be sterilised. It is important to buy sturdy bowls since anything is in danger of being chewed by puppy teeth and you do not want your dog to be constantly chewing apart his bowl (for his safety and for your wallet!).

CLEANING SUPPLIES

Until a pup is housetrained you will be doing a lot of cleaning. Accidents will occur, which is okay in the beginning because he does not know any better. All you can do is clean up any 'accidents.' Old rags, towels, newspapers and a safe disinfectant are good to have on hand.

BEYOND THE BASICS

The items previously discussed are the bare necessities. You will find out what else you need as you go along—grooming supplies, flea/tick protection, baby gates to partition a room, etc. These things will vary depending on your situation but it is important that you have everything you need to feed and make your Staffordshire comfortable in his first few days at home.

PUPPY-PROOFING YOUR HOME
Aside from making sure that your Staffordshire will be comfortable in your home, you also have to make sure that your home is safe for your Staffordshire. This means taking precautions that your pup will not get into anything he should not get into and that there is nothing within his reach that may harm him should he sniff it, chew it, inspect it, etc. This probably seems obvious since, while you are primarily concerned with your pup's safety, at the same time you do not want your belongings to be ruined. Breakables should be placed out of reach if your dog is to have full run of the house. If he is to be limited to certain places within the house, keep any potentially dangerous items in the 'off-limits' areas. An electrical cord can pose a danger should the puppy decide to taste it—and who is going to convince a pup that it would not make a great chew toy? Cords should be fastened tightly against the wall. If your dog is going to spend time in a crate, make sure that there is nothing near his crate that he can reach if he sticks his curious little nose or paws through the openings. Just as you would with a child, keep all household cleaners and chemicals

DID YOU KNOW?
Two important documents you will get from the breeder are the pup's pedigree and registration papers. The breeder should register the litter and each pup with The Kennel Club, and it is necessary for you to have the paperwork if you plan on showing or breeding in the future.

Make sure you know the breeder's intentions on which type of registration he will obtain for the pup. There are limited registrations which may prohibit the dog from being shown or from competing in non-conformation trials such as Working or Agility if the breeder feels that the pup is not of sufficient quality to do so. There is also a type of registration that will permit the dog in non-conformation competition only.

If your dog is registered with a Kennel-Club-recognised breed club, then you can register the pup with The Kennel Club yourself. Your breeder can assist you with the specifics of the registration process.

where the pup cannot get to them.

It is also important to make sure that the outside of your home is safe. Of course your puppy should never be unsupervised, but a pup let loose in the garden will want to run and explore, and he should be granted that freedom. Do not let a fence give you a false sense of security; you would be surprised how crafty (and persistent) a dog can be in figuring out

51

Be certain to have your new puppy checked by your veterinary surgeon before you take him home.

how to dig under and squeeze his way through small holes, or to jump or climb over a fence. The remedy is to make the fence high enough so that it really is impossible for your dog to get over it (about 3 metres should suffice), and well embedded into the ground. Be sure to repair or secure any gaps in the fence. Check the fence periodically to ensure that it is in good shape and make repairs as needed; a very determined pup may return to the same spot to 'work on it' until he is able to get through.

FIRST TRIP TO THE VET
You have picked out your puppy, and your home and family are ready. Now all you have to do is pick up your Staffordshire from the breeder and the fun begins, right? Well...not so fast.

Something else you need to prepare is your pup's first trip to the veterinary surgeon. Perhaps the breeder can recommend someone in the area that specialises in Staffordshires, or maybe you know some other Staffordshire owners who can suggest a good vet. Either way, you should have an appointment arranged for your pup before you pick him up and plan on taking him for a checkup before bringing him home.

The pup's first visit will consist of an overall examination to make sure that the pup does not have any problems that are not apparent to the eye. The veterinary surgeon will also set up

DID YOU KNOW?
Grooming tools, collars, leashes, dog beds and, of course, toys will be an expense to you when you first obtain your pup, and the cost will trickle on throughout your dog's lifetime. If your puppy damages or destroys your possessions (as most puppies surely will!) or something belonging to a neighbour, you can calculate additional expense. There is also flea and pest control, which every dog owner faces more than once. You must be able to handle the financial responsibility of owning a dog.

a schedule for the pup's vaccinations; the breeder will inform you of which ones the pup has already received and the vet can continue from there.

Be aware of the pup's growth and adjust the collar regularly. It seems that the puppy is growing on a daily basis!

INTRODUCTION TO THE FAMILY

Everyone in the house will be excited about the puppy coming home and will want to pet him and play with him, but it is best to make the introduction low-key so as not to overwhelm the puppy. He is apprehensive already. It is the first time he has been separated from his mother and the breeder, and the ride to your home is likely the first time he has been in an auto. The last thing

DID YOU KNOW?

An important consideration to be discussed is the sex of your puppy. For a family companion, a Staffordshire bitch is the best choice, considering the female's inbred concern for all young creatures and her accompanying tolerance and patience. If you do not intend to spay your pet when she has matured or is well over her growing period, then extra care is required during the times of her heat.

you want to do is smother him, as this will only frighten him further. This is not to say that human contact is not extremely necessary at this stage, because this is the time when a connection between the pup and his human family is formed. Gentle petting and soothing words should help console him, as well as just putting him down and letting him explore on his own (under your watchful eye, of course).

The pup may approach the family members or may busy

himself with exploring for awhile. Gradually, each person should spend some time with the pup, one at a time, crouching down to get as close to the pup's level as possible and letting him sniff their hands and petting him gently. He definitely needs human attention and he needs to be touched—this is how to form an immediate bond. Just remember that the pup is experiencing a lot of things for the first time, at the same time. There are new people, new noises, new smells, and new things to investigate; so be gentle, be affectionate, and be as comforting as you can be.

YOUR PUP'S FIRST NIGHT HOME

You have travelled home with your new charge safely in his basket or crate. He's been to the vet for a thorough check-over; he's been weighed, his papers examined; perhaps he's even been vaccinated and wormed as well. He's met the family, licked the

The toughest night with your Staffordshire puppy will be the first night at home, for both the puppy and the family.

whole family, including the excited children and the less-than-happy cat. He's explored his area, his new bed, the garden and anywhere else he's been permit-

DID YOU KNOW?

The electrical fencing system which forms an invisible fence works on a battery-operated collar that shocks the dog if it gets too close to the buried (or elevated) wire. There are some people who think very highly of this system of controlling a dog's wandering. Keep in mind that the collar has batteries. For safety's sake, replace the batteries every month with the best quality batteries available.

ted. He's eaten his first meal at home and relieved himself in the proper place. He's heard lots of new sounds, smelled new friends and seen more of the outside world than ever before.

That was the just the first day! He's tuckered out and is ready for bed...or so you think!

It's puppy's first night and you are ready to say 'Good night'—keep in mind that this is puppy's first night ever to be sleeping alone. His dam and littermates are no longer at paw's length and he's a bit scared, cold and lonely. Be reassuring to your new family member. This is not the time to spoil him and give in to his inevitable whining.

Puppies whine. They whine to let the others know where they

are and hopefully to get company out of it. Place your pup in his new bed or crate in his room and close the door. Mercifully, he may fall asleep without a peep. If the inevitable occurs, ignore the whining; he is fine. Be strong and keep his interest in mind. Do not allow your heart to become guilty and visit the pup. He will fall asleep.

Many breeders recommend placing a piece of bedding from his former homestead in his new bed so that he recognises the scent of his littermates. Others still advise placing a hot water bottle in his bed for warmth. This latter may be a good idea provided the pup doesn't attempt to suckle—

> **DID YOU KNOW?**
> You will probably start feeding your Staffordshire pup the same food that he has been getting from the breeder; the breeder should give you a few days' supply to start you off. Although you should not give your pup too many treats, you will want to have puppy treats on hand for coaxing, training, rewards, etc. Be careful, though, as a small pup's calorie requirements are relatively low and a few treats can add up to almost a full day's worth of calories without the required nutrition.

he'll get good and wet and may not fall asleep so fast.

Puppy's first night can be somewhat stressful for the pup and his new family. Remember that you are setting the tone of nighttime at your house. Unless you want to play with your pup every evening at 10 p.m., midnight and 2 a.m., don't initiate the habit. Your family will thank you, and so will your pup!

PREVENTING PUPPY PROBLEMS
SOCIALISATION
Now that you have done all of the preparatory work and have helped your pup get accustomed to his new home and family, it is about time for you to have some fun! Socialising your Staffordshire pup gives you the opportunity to show off your new friend, and your pup

Puppies require attention and instruction. The first few days in your home should be completely under control. Do not overwhelm the puppy with too many new experiences and people all at once.

55

gets to reap the benefits of being an adorable furry creature that people will coo over, want to pet and, in general, think is absolutely precious!

Besides getting to know his new family, your puppy should be exposed to other people, animals and situations. This will help him become well adjusted as he grows up and less prone to being timid or fearful of the new things he will encounter. Your pup's socialisation began at the breeder's but now it is your responsibility to

DID YOU KNOW?

Many plants can be toxic to dogs. If you see your dog carrying a piece of vegetation in his mouth, approach him in a quiet, disinterested manner, avoid eye contact, pet him and gradually remove the plant from his mouth. Alternatively, offer him a treat and maybe he'll drop the plant on his own accord. Be sure no toxic plants are growing in your own garden.

continue it. The socialisation he receives up until the age of 12 weeks is the most critical, as this is the time when he forms his impressions of the outside world. Be especially careful during the eight-to-ten-week period, also known as the fear period. The interaction he receives during this time should be gentle and reassur-

ing. Lack of socialisation can manifest itself in fear and aggression as the dog grows up. He needs lots of human contact, affection, handling and exposure to other animals.

Once your pup has received his necessary vaccinations, feel free to take him out and about (on his lead, of course). Take him around the neighbourhood, take him on your daily errands, let people pet him, let him meet other dogs and pets, etc. Puppies do not have to try to make friends; there will be no shortage of people who will want to introduce themselves. Just make sure that you carefully supervise each meeting. If the neighbourhood children want to say hello, for example, that is great—children and pups most often make great companions.

to you! Your pup's intuitive quest for dominance, coupled with the fact that it is nearly impossible to look at an adorable Staffordshire pup, with his 'puppy-dog' eyes not cave in, give the pup almost an unfair advantage in getting the upper hand! A pup will definitely test the waters to see what he can and cannot do. Do not give in to those pleading eyes—stand your ground when it comes to disciplining the pup and make sure that all family members do

Staffordshire Bull Terrier puppies learn about the world through their association with their dam and littermates. Breeders allow pups to be handled by people to further the pup's socialisation.

> **DID YOU KNOW?**
> Training your puppy takes much patience and can be frustrating at times, but you should see results from your efforts. If you have a puppy that seems untrainable, take him to a trainer or behaviourist. The dog may have a personality problem that requires the help of a professional, or perhaps you need help in learning how to train your dog.

Sometimes an excited child can unintentionally handle a pup too roughly, or an overzealous pup can playfully nip a little too hard. You want to make socialisation experiences positive ones. What a pup learns during this very formative stage will impact his attitude toward future encounters. You want your dog to be comfortable around everyone. A pup that has a bad experience with a child may grow up to be a dog that is shy around or aggressive toward children.

CONSISTENCY IN TRAINING
Dogs, being pack animals, naturally need a leader, or else they try to establish dominance in their packs. When you bring a dog into your family, the choice of who becomes the leader and who becomes the 'pack' is entirely up

the same. It will only confuse the pup when Mother tells him to get off the couch when he is used to sitting up there with Father to watch the nightly news. Avoid discrepancies by having all members of the household decide on the rules before the pup even comes home…and be consistent in enforcing them! Early training shapes the dog's personality, so you cannot be unclear in what you expect.

Providing play things, like safe chew toys, from an early age helps channel the pups' chewing instincts in positive ways.

COMMON PUPPY PROBLEMS

The best way to prevent problems is to be proactive in stopping an undesirable behaviour as soon as it starts. The old saying 'You can't teach an old dog new tricks' does not necessarily hold true, but it is true that it is much easier to discourage bad behaviour in a young developing pup than to wait until the pup's bad behaviour becomes the adult dog's bad habit.

Do not give in to pleading eyes.

There are some problems that are especially prevalent in puppies as they develop.

NIPPING

As puppies start to teethe, they feel the need to sink their teeth into anything available…unfortu-

DID YOU KNOW?

Thorough socialisation includes not only meeting new people but also being introduced to new experiences such as riding in the auto, having his coat brushed, hearing the television, walking in a crowd—the list is endless. The more your pup experiences, and the more positive the experiences are, the less of a shock and the less scary it will be for your pup to encounter new things.

nately that includes your fingers, arms, hair, and toes. You may find this behaviour cute for the first five seconds…until you feel just how sharp those puppy teeth are. This is something you want to discourage immediately and consistently with a firm 'No!' (or whatever number of firm 'No's' it takes for him to understand that you mean business). Then replace your finger with an appropriate chew toy. While this behaviour is merely annoying when the dog is young, it can become dangerous as your Staffordshire's adult teeth grow in and his jaws develop, and he continues to think it is okay to gnaw on human appendages. You do not want to take a chance with a Staffordshire as this is a breed whose jaws become very strong. He does not mean any harm with a friendly nip, but he also does not know his own strength.

CRYING/WHINING

Your pup will often cry, whine, whimper, howl or make some type of commotion when he is left alone. This is basically his way of calling out for attention to make sure that you know he is there and that you have not forgotten about him. He feels insecure when he is left alone, when you are out of the house and he is in his crate or when you are in another part of the house and he cannot see you. The noise he is making is an expression of the anxiety he feels at being alone, so he needs to be taught that being alone is okay. You are not actually training the dog to stop making noise, you are training him to feel comfortable when he is alone and thus removing the need for him to make the noise. This is where the crate filled with cosy blankets and toys comes in handy. You want to know that he is safe when you are not there to supervise, and you know that he will be safe in his

Expect your new Staff puppy to cry for his littermates and mother during his first night in your home. This traumatic change in his life requires the owner's sensitivity.

crate rather than roaming freely about the house. In order for the pup to stay in his crate without making a fuss, he needs to be comfortable in his crate. On that note, it is extremely important that the crate is never used as a form of punishment, or the pup will have a negative association with the crate.

Accustom the pup to the crate in short, gradually increasing time intervals in which you put him in the crate, maybe with a treat, and stay in the room with him. If he cries or makes a fuss, do not go to him, but stay in his sight. Gradually he will realise that staying in his crate is all right without your help, and it will not be so traumatic for him when you are not around. You may want to leave the radio on softly when you leave the house; the sound of human voices may be comforting to him.

It is very important for your children to *gently* handle your new Staff puppy. They must be instructed to be kind and gentle to all living things.

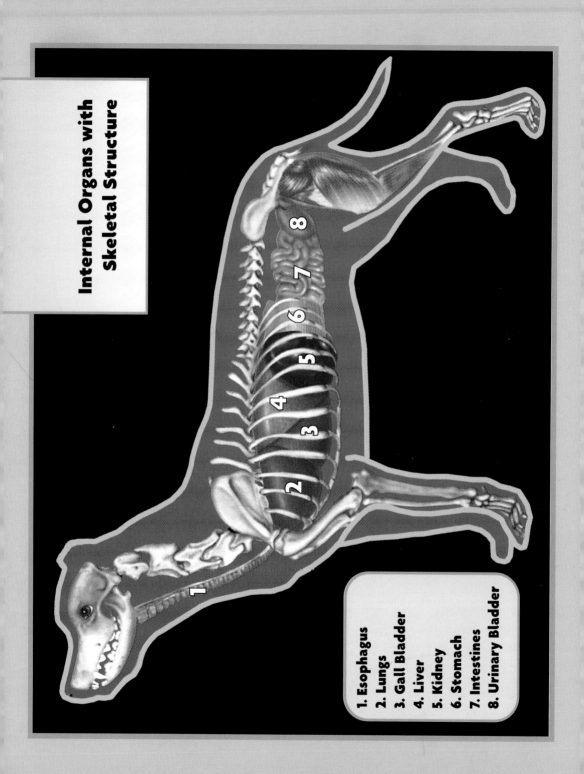

Internal Organs with Skeletal Structure

1. Esophagus
2. Lungs
3. Gall Bladder
4. Liver
5. Kidney
6. Stomach
7. Intestines
8. Urinary Bladder

DIETARY AND FEEDING CONSIDERATIONS

You have probably heard it a thousand times, 'you are what you eat.' Believe it or not, it's very true. Dogs are what you feed them because they have

little choice in the matter. Even those people who truly want to feed their dogs the best often cannot do so because they do not know which foods are best for their dogs.

Dog foods are produced in three basic types: dry, semi-moist and canned or tinned. Dry foods are for the cost conscious because they are much less expensive than semi-moist and canned. Dry foods contain the least fat and the most preservatives. Most tinned foods are 60 to 70 percent water, while semi-moist foods are so full of sugar that they are the least preferred by owners, though

DID YOU KNOW?

Selecting the best dry dog food is difficult. There is no majority consensus among veterinary scientists as to the value of nutrient analyses (protein, fat, fibre, moisture, ash, cholesterol, minerals, etc.). All agree that feeding trials are what matters, but you also have to consider the individual dog. Its weight, age, activity and what pleases its taste, all must be considered. It is probably best to take the advice of your veterinary surgeon. Every dog's dietary requirements vary, even during the lifetime of a particular dog.

If your dog is fed a good dry food, it does not require supplements of meat or vegetables. Dogs do appreciate a little variety in their diets so you may choose to stay with the same brand, but vary the flavour. Alternatively you may wish to add a little flavoured stock to give a difference to the taste.

Staffordshire Bull Terrier puppies nurse from their dam for about six weeks, after which period the breeder begins to wean the pups from the mother's milk supply.

61

dogs welcome them (as a child does sweets).

Three stages of development must be considered when selecting a diet for your dog: the puppy stage, the mid-age or adult stage and the senior age or geriatric stage.

PUPPY STAGE

Puppies have a natural instinct to suck milk from their mother's breasts. They should exhibit this behaviour from the first day of their lives. If they don't suckle within a few hours you should attempt to put them onto their mother's nipple. Their failure to feed means you have to feed them yourself under the advice and guidance of a

Staffordshire puppy diets should be balanced for your puppy's needs. It is usually not necessary to add vitamin and mineral supplements if the puppy is normal and healthy.

Your Staffordshire must have a balanced diet at every age.

veterinary surgeon. This will involve a baby bottle and a special formula. Their mother's milk is much better than any formula because it contains colostrum, a sort of antibiotic milk which protects the puppy during the first eight to ten weeks of their lives.

Puppies should be allowed to nurse for six weeks and

they should be slowly weaned away from their mother by introducing small portions of tinned meat after they are about one month old. Then dry food is gradually added to the puppies' portions over the next few weeks.

By the time they are eight

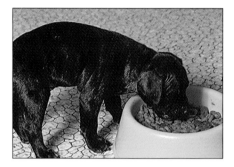

weeks old, they should be completely weaned and fed solely a puppy dry food. During this weaning period, their diet is most important as the puppy grows fastest during its first year of life. Growth foods can be recommended by your veterinary surgeon and the puppy should be kept on this diet for up to 18 months.

Puppy diets should be balanced for your dog's needs, and supplements of vitamins, minerals and protein should not be necessary.

ADULT DIETS

A dog is considered an adult when it has stopped growing in height and/or length. Do not consider the dog's weight when the decision is made to switch from a puppy diet to a maintenance diet. Again you should rely upon your veterinary surgeon to recommend an acceptable maintenance diet. Major dog food manufacturers specialise in this type of food and it is just necessary for you to select the one best suited to your dog's needs. Active dogs may have different requirements than sedate dogs.

Adult Staffs have different dietary needs than puppies. Breeding dams may require diets different than males.

> **DID YOU KNOW?**
> You must store your dry dog food carefully. Open packages of dog food quickly lose their vitamin value, usually within 90 days of being opened. Mould spores and vermin could also contaminate the food.

A Staffordshire reaches adulthood between 18 and 24 months of age, though dogs will reach their full height by one year of age and 'fill out' for the next 6 to 12 months.

DIETS FOR SENIOR DOGS
As dogs get older, their metabolism changes. The older dog usually exercises less, moves more slowly and sleeps more. This change in lifestyle and physiological performance requires a change in diet. Since these changes

take place slowly, they might not be recognisable. What is easily recognisable is weight gain. By continually feeding your dog an adult maintenance diet when it is slowing down metabolically, your dog will gain weight. Obesity in an older dog compounds the health problems that already accompany old age.

As your dog gets older, few of his organs function up to par. The kidneys slow down and the intestines become less efficient. These age-related factors are best handled

> **DID YOU KNOW?**
> A good test for proper diet is the colour, odour, and firmness of your dog's stool. A healthy dog usually produces three semi-hard stools per day. The stools should have no unpleasant odour. They should be the same colour from excretion to excretion.

63

All Staffordshires require exercise. They are a very active breed and they do not lend themselves well to a sedentary life.

with a change in diet and a change in feeding schedule to give smaller portions that are more easily digested.

There is no single best diet for every older dog. While many dogs do well on light or senior diets, other dogs do better on puppy diets or other special premium diets such as lamb and rice.

Be sensitive to your senior Staffordshire's diet and this will help control other problems that may arise with your old friend.

DID YOU KNOW?

Dog food must be at room temperature, neither too hot nor too cold. Fresh water, changed daily and served in a clean bowl, is mandatory, especially when feeding dry food.

Never feed your dog from the table while you are eating. Never feed your dog left-overs from your own meal. They usually contain too much fat and too much seasoning.

Dogs must chew their food. Hard pellets are excellent; soups and slurries are to be avoided.

Don't add left-overs or any extras to normal dog food. The normal food is usually balanced and adding something extra destroys the balance.

Except for age-related changes, dogs do not require dietary variations. They should be fed the same diet, day after day, without their becoming bored or ill.

WATER

Just as your dog needs proper nutrition from his food, water is an essential "nutrient" as well. Water keeps the dog's body properly hydrated and promotes normal function of the body's systems. During housebreaking it is necessary to keep an eye on how much water your Staffordshire is drinking, but once he is reliably trained he should have access to clean fresh water at all times. Make sure that the dog's water bowl is clean, and change the water often.

EXERCISE

All dogs require some form of exercise, regardless of breed. A sedentary lifestyle is as

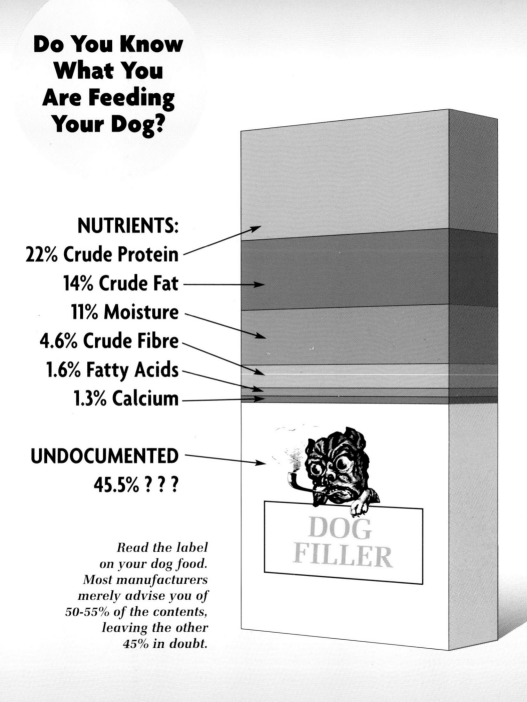

DID YOU KNOW?

Many adult diets are based on grain. There is nothing wrong with this as long as it does not contain soy meal. Diets based on soy often cause flatulence (passing gas).

Grain-based diets are almost always the least expensive and a good grain diet is just as good as the most expensive diet containing animal protein.

There are many cases, however, when your dog might require a special diet. These special requirements should only be recommended by your veterinary surgeon.

harmful to a dog as it is to a person. The Staffordshire happens to be an above-active breed that requires more exercise than most breeds. Regular walks, play sessions in the garden, or letting the dog run free in the garden under your supervision are all sufficient forms of exercise for

Your Staff must ALWAYS have fresh water available in a separate water bowl. The water should be changed daily and the bowl cleaned at the same time.

the Staffordshire. For those who are more ambitious, you will find that your Staffordshire will be able to keep up with you on extra long walks or the morning run. Not only is exercise essential to keep the dog's body fit, it is essential to his mental well-being. A bored dog will find something to do, which often manifests itself in some type of destructive behaviour. In this sense, it is essential for the owner's mental well-being as well!

GROOMING

BRUSHING

A natural bristle brush or a hound glove can be used for regular routine brushing. Daily brushing is effective for removing dead hair and stimulating the dog's natural oils to add shine and a healthy look to the coat. Although the Staffordshire's coat is short and close, it does require a five-minute once-over to keep it looking its shiny best. Regular grooming sessions are also a good way to spend time with your dog. Many dogs grow to like the feel of being brushed and will enjoy the daily routine.

BATHING

Dogs do not need to be bathed as often as humans, but

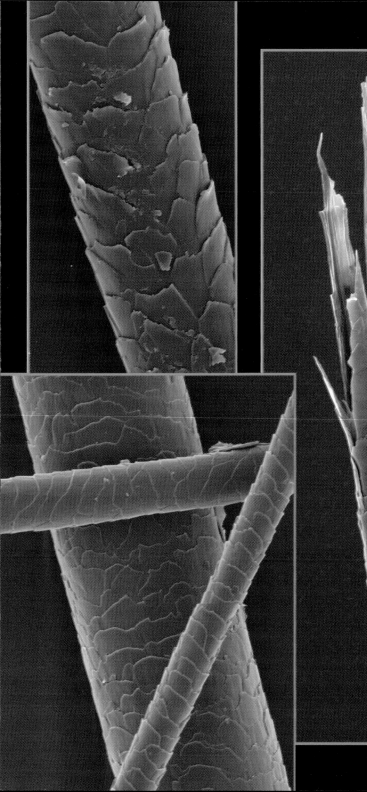

Typical flat-coated breed hairs, greatly enlarged with a scanning electron microscope, shows an unhealthy hair (top left), a healthy thick top coat hair and a thin undercoat hair (bottom left). The hair on the right shows split ends possibly due to too much sun or strong shampooing. S.E.M.s by Dr. Dennis Kunkel, University of Hawaii.

DID YOU KNOW?
Once you are sure that the dog is thoroughly rinsed, squeeze the excess water out of the coat with your hand and dry him with a heavy towel. You may choose to blow-dry his coat or just let it dry naturally. In cold weather, never allow your dog outside with a wet coat.
There are 'dry bath' products on the market, which are sprays and powders intended for spot cleaning, that can be used between regular baths, if necessary. They are not substitutes for regular baths, but they are easy to use for touch-ups as they do not require rinsing.

the dog's coat and work it into a good lather. You should purchase a shampoo that is made for dogs. Do not use a product made for human hair. Wash the head last; you do not want shampoo to drip into the dog's eyes while you are washing the rest of his body. Work the shampoo all the way down to the skin. You can use this opportunity to check the skin for any bumps, bites or other abnormalities. Do not neglect any area of the body—get all of the hard-to-reach places.

Once the dog has been thoroughly shampooed, he requires an equally thorough rinsing. Shampoo left in the coat can be irritating to the skin. Protect his eyes from the shampoo by

regular bathing is essential for healthy skin and a healthy, shiny coat. Again, like most anything, if you accustom your pup to being bathed as a puppy, it will be second nature by the time he grows up. You want your dog to be at ease in the bath or else it could end up a wet, soapy, messy ordeal for both of you!

Make sure that your dog has a good non-slip surface to stand on. Begin by wetting the dog's coat. A shower or hose attachment is necessary for thoroughly wetting and rinsing the coat. Check the water temperature to make sure that it is neither too hot nor too cold.

Next, apply shampoo to

DID YOU KNOW?
The use of human soap products like shampoo, bubble bath and soap can be damaging to a dog's coat and skin. Human products are too strong and remove the protective oils coating the dog's hair and skin (making him water-resistant). Use only shampoo made especially for dogs and you may like to use a medicated shampoo which will always help to keep external parasites at bay.

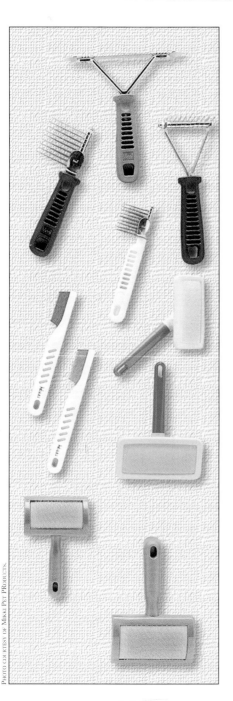

shielding them with your hand and directing the flow of water in the opposite direction. You should also avoid getting water in the ear canal. Be prepared for your dog to shake out his coat—you might want to stand back, but make sure you have a hold on the dog to keep him from running through the house.

Your local pet shop can offer a wide range of grooming tools. Fortunately, the Staffordshire requires little grooming besides the regular brushing, ear cleaning and nail clipping.

EAR CLEANING

The ears should be kept clean and any excess hair inside the ear should be trimmed. Ears

Your Staffordshire puppy's ears should be cleaned regularly, perhaps once a week. During the cleaning you should be alert for any signs of irritation or infection.

can be cleaned with a cotton ball and special cleaner or ear powder made especially for dogs. Be on the lookout for any signs of infection or ear mite infestation. If your Staffordshire has been shaking his head or scratching at his ears frequently, this usually indicates a problem. If his ears have an unusual odour, this is

Clipping is best accomplished with a special dog nail clipper. Accustom the young pup to having its feet touched and nails clipped so that the dog doesn't object when it is older.

a sure sign of mite infestation or infection, and a signal to have his ears checked by the veterinary surgeon.

NAIL CLIPPING

Your Staffordshire should be accustomed to having his nails trimmed at an early age, since it will be part of your maintenance routine throughout his life. Not only does it look nicer, but a dog with long nails can cause injury if he jumps up or if he scratches someone unintentionally. Also, a long nail has a better chance of ripping and bleeding, or causing the feet to spread. A good rule of thumb is if you can hear your dog's nails clicking on the floor when he walks, his nails are too long.

It is relatively simple to clip a white, transparent nail, without cutting the quick, the vein that goes through the nail. A dark nail poses problems that are best handled by cutting only the sharp tip off the nail on a frequent basis.

Grooming your Staffordshire should be a pleasure, not a chore.

Before you start cutting, make sure you can identify the 'quick' in each nail. The quick is a blood vessel that runs through the centre of each nail and grows rather close to the end. It will bleed if accidentally cut, which will be quite painful for the dog as it contains nerve endings. Keep some type of clotting agent on hand, such as a styptic pencil or styptic powder (the type used for shaving). This will stop the bleeding quickly

Walking on hard surfaces naturally wears down a dog's nails, thus the dog will need to have his nails clipped less frequently.

71

DID YOU KNOW?

A dog that spends a lot of time outside on a hard surface such as cement or pavement will have his nails naturally worn down and may not need to have them trimmed as often, except maybe in the colder months when he is not outside as much. Regardless, it is best to get your dog accustomed to this procedure at an early age so that he is used to it. Some dogs are especially sensitive about having their feet touched, but if a dog has experienced it since he was young, he should not be bothered by it.

when applied to the end of the cut nail. Do not panic if this happens, just stop the bleeding and talk soothingly to your dog. Once he has calmed down, move on to the next nail. It is better to clip a little at a time, particularly with black-nailed dogs.

Hold your pup steady as you begin trimming his nails; you do not want him to make any sudden movements or run away. Talk to him soothingly and stroke his fur as you clip. Holding his foot in your hand, simply take off the end of each nail in one quick clip. You can purchase nail clippers that are specially made for dogs; you can probably find them wherever you buy pet or grooming supplies.

Driving with your Staff in the rear of the vehicle is extremely unsafe. Even if tethered, there is still a big danger of the dog's falling out and becoming injured.

TRAVELLING WITH YOUR DOG

AUTOMOBILE TRAVEL

You should accustom your Staffordshire to riding in an car at an early age. You may or may not take him in the car often, but at the very least he will need to go to the vet and you do not want these trips to be traumatic for the dog or a big hassle for you. The safest way for a dog to ride in the car is in his crate. If he uses a fibreglass crate in the house, you can use the same crate for travel. Wire crates can be used for travel, but fibreglass or wooden crates are safer. If you have a wire crate in the house, consider purchasing an appropriately sized fibreglass or wooden crate for travelling.

Put the pup in the crate and see how he reacts. If he

seems uneasy, you can have a passenger hold him on his lap while you drive. Another option is a specially made safety harness for dogs, which straps the dog in much like a seat belt. Do not let the dog roam loose in the vehicle—this is very dangerous! If you should stop short, your dog can be thrown and injured. If the dog starts climbing on you and pestering you while you are driving, you will not be able to concentrate on the road. It is an unsafe situation for everyone—human and canine.

For long trips, be prepared to stop to let the dog relieve himself. Bring along whatever you need to clean up after him. You should bring along some old towels and rags, should he have an accident in the car or become carsick.

DID YOU KNOW?

When travelling, never let your dog off-lead in a strange area. Your dog could run away out of fear or decide to chase a passing chipmunk or cat or simply want to stretch his legs without restriction—you might never see your canine friend again.

AIR TRAVEL

If bringing your dog on a flight, you will have to contact the airline to make special arrangements. It is rather common for dogs to travel by air, but advance permission is usually required. The dog will be required to travel in a fibreglass crate; you may be able to use your own or the airline can usually supply one. To help the dog be at ease, put one of his favourite toys in the crate with him. Do not feed the dog for at least six hours before the trip to minimise his need to relieve

A Staffordshire Bull Terrier is not considered an adult until he stops growing.

himself. However, certain regulations specify that water must always be made available to the dog in the crate.

Make sure your dog is properly identified and that your contact information appears on his ID tags and on his crate. Animals travel in a different area of the plane than human passengers, and, although transporting animals is routine for large airlines, there is always the slight risk of getting separated from your dog.

BOARDING

So you want to take a family holiday—and you want to include all members of the family. You would probably make arrangements for accommodations ahead of time anyway, but this is especially important when travelling with a dog. You do not want to make an overnight stop at the only place around for miles and find out that they do not allow dogs. Also, you do not want to reserve a place for your family without mentioning that you are bringing a dog because if it is against their policy you may not have a place to stay.

Alternatively, if you are travelling and choose not to bring your Staffordshire, you will have to make arrangements for him while you are away. Some options are to bring him to a neighbour's house to stay while you are gone, to have a trusted neighbour stop by often or stay at your house, or bring your dog to a reputable boarding kennel. If you choose to board him at a kennel, you should stop by to see the facility and where the dogs are kept to make sure that it is clean. Talk to some of the

If your Staff is accustomed to spending all its time with you, the dog may not adjust very well to a boarding kennel when you decide to take a holiday.

employees and see how they treat the dogs—do they spend time with the dogs, play with them, exercise them, etc.? You know that your Staffordshire will not be happy unless he gets regular activity. Also find out the kennel's policy on

vaccinations and what they require. This is for all of the dogs' safety, since when dogs are kept together, there is a greater risk of diseases being passed from dog to dog.

DID YOU KNOW?
You have a valuable dog. If the dog is lost or stolen you would undoubtedly become extremely upset. If you encounter a lost dog, notify the police or the local animal shelter.

Staff puppies can be tattooed as young as ten weeks of age. The tattoo is commonly done on the inside of their thighs. This photo has been retouched for emphasis.

DID YOU KNOW?

As puppies become more and more expensive, especially those puppies of high quality for showing and/or breeding, they have a greater chance of being stolen. The usual collar dog tag is, of course, easily removed. But there are two techniques which are becoming widely utilised for identification.

The puppy microchip implantation involves the injection of a small microchip, about the size of a corn kernel, under the skin of the dog. If your dog shows up at a clinic or shelter, or is offered for resale under less than savory circumstances, it can be positively identified by the microchip. The microchip is scanned and a registry quickly identifies you as the owner. This is not only protection against theft, but should the dog run away or go chasing a varmint and get lost, you have a fair chance of getting it back.

Tattooing is done on various parts of the dog, from its belly to its cheeks. The number tattooed can be your telephone number or any other number which you can easily memorise. When professional dog thieves see a tattooed dog, they usually lose interest in it. Both microchipping and tattooing can be done at your local veterinary clinic. For the safety of our dogs, no laboratory facility or dog broker will accept a tattooed dog as stock.

IDENTIFICATION

Your Staffordshire is your valued companion and friend. That is why you always keep a close eye on him and you have made sure that he cannot escape from the garden or wriggle out of his collar and run away from you. However, accidents can happen and there may come a time when your dog unexpectedly gets separated from you. If this unfortunate event should occur, the first thing on your mind will be finding him. Proper identification, including an ID tag, a tattoo and possibly a microchip, will increase the chances of his being returned to you safely and quickly.

75

HOUSEBREAKING AND TRAINING YOUR
Staffordshire Bull Terrier

Living with an untrained dog is a lot like owning a piano that you do not know how to play—it is a nice object to look at but it does not do much more than that to bring you pleasure. Now try taking piano lessons and suddenly the piano comes alive and brings forth magical sounds and rhythms that set your heart singing and your body swaying.

The same is true with your Staffordshire Bull Terrier. At first you enjoy seeing him around the house. He does not do much with you other than to need food, water and exercise. Come to think of it, he does not bring you much joy, either. He is a big responsibility with a very small return. Often he develops unacceptable behaviours that annoy and/or infuriate you to say nothing of bad habits that may end up costing you great sums of money. Not a good thing!

Now train your Staffordshire. Enrol in an obedience class. Teach him good manners as you learn how and why he behaves the way he does. Find out how to communicate with your dog and how to recognise and understand his communications with you. Suddenly the dog takes on a new role in your life—he is smart, interesting, well behaved and fun to be with. He demonstrates his bond of devotion to you daily. In other words, your Staffordshire does wonders for your ego because he constantly reminds you that you are not only his leader, you are his hero! Miraculous things have happened—you have a wonderful dog (even your family and friends have noticed the

(opposite page) As cute and innocent as this Staffordshire pup looks, he can certainly cause a lot of trouble if not properly trained!

Staffordshire Bull Terriers are extremely intelligent dogs. They are readily trained and can bring much pleasure and happiness into the lives of their keepers.

77

transformation!) and you feel good about yourself.

Those involved with teaching dog obedience and counselling owners about their dogs' behaviour have discovered some interesting facts about dog ownership. For example, training dogs when they are puppies results in the highest rate of success in developing well-mannered and well-adjusted adult dogs. Training an older dog, from six months to six years of age, can produce almost equal results providing that the owner

Puppies are most trainable from 2 to 4 months of age.

accepts the dog's slower rate of learning capability and is willing to work patiently to help the dog succeed at developing to his fullest potential. Unfortunately many owners of untrained adult dogs lack the patience factor, so they do not persist until their dogs are successful at learning particular behaviours.

Training a puppy aged 8 to 16 weeks (20 weeks at the most) is like working with a dry sponge in a pool of water. The pup soaks up whatever you

DID YOU KNOW?

If you start with a normal, healthy dog and give him time, patience and some carefully executed lessons, you will reap the rewards of that training for the life of the dog. And what a life it will be! The two of you will find immeasurable pleasure in the companionship you have built together with love, respect and understanding. Good luck and enjoy!

show him and constantly looks for more things to do and learn. At this early age, his body is not yet producing hormones, and therein lies the reason for such a high rate of success. Without hormones, he is focused on his owners and not particularly interested in investigating other places, dogs, people, etc. You are his leader: his provider of food, water, shelter and security. He latches onto you and wants to stay close. He will usually follow you from room to room, will

DID YOU KNOW?

Your dog is actually training you at the same time you are training him. Dogs do things to get attention. They usually repeat whatever succeeds in getting your attention.

DID YOU KNOW?

Dogs do not understand our language. They can be trained to react to a certain sound, at a certain volume. If you say 'No, Oliver' in a very soft pleasant voice it will not have the same meaning as 'No, Oliver!!' when you shout it as loud as you can. You should never use the dog's name during a reprimand, just the command NO!! Since dogs don't understand words, comics use dogs trained with opposite meanings to the world. Thus, when the comic commands his dog to SIT the dog will stand up; and vice versa.

During training, such as this sitting exercise, you must maintain eye contact with your Staff. If the dog consistently refuses to look you in the eye, you will have a problem training and controlling the dog.

this behaviour becomes a problem, the owner has two choices: get rid of the dog or train him. It is strongly urged that you choose the latter option.

Occasionally there are no classes available within a

not let you out of his sight when you are outdoors with him, and respond in like manner to the people and animals you encounter. If you greet a friend warmly, he will be happy to greet the person as well. If, however, you are hesitant, even anxious, about the approach of a stranger, he will respond accordingly.

Once the puppy begins to produce hormones, his natural curiosity emerges and he begins to investigate the world around him. It is at this time when you may notice that the untrained dog begins to wander away from you and even ignore your commands to stay close. When

DID YOU KNOW?

The puppy should also have regular play and exercise sessions when he is with you or a family member. Exercise for a very young puppy can consist of a short walk around the house or garden. Playing can include fetching games with a large ball or an old sock with a knot tied in the middle. (All puppies teethe and need soft things upon which to chew.) Remember to restrict play periods to indoors within his living area (the family room for example) until he is completely housetrained.

79

reasonable distance from the owner's home. Sometimes there are classes available but the tuition is too costly. Whatever the circumstances, the solution to the problem of lack of lesson availability lies within the pages of this book.

This chapter is devoted to helping you train your Staffordshire at home. If the recommended procedures are followed faithfully, you may expect positive results that will prove rewarding to both you and your dog.

Whether your Staffordshire is a puppy or a mature adult, the methods of teaching and the techniques we use in training basic behaviours are the same. After all, no dog, whether puppy or adult, likes harsh or inhumane methods. All creatures, however, respond

HOW MANY TIMES A DAY?

AGE	RELIEF TRIPS
To 14 weeks	10
14–22 weeks	8
22–32 weeks	6
Adulthood (dog stops growing)	4

These are estimates, of course, but they are a guide as to the MINIMUM opportunities a dog should have each day to relieve itself.

favourably to gentle motivational methods and sincere praise and encouragement. Now let us get started.

HOUSEBREAKING
You can train a puppy to relieve itself wherever you choose. For example, city dwellers often train their puppies to relieve themselves in the gutter because large plots of grass are not readily available. Suburbanites, on the other hand, usually have gardens to accommodate their dogs' needs.

Outdoor training includes such surfaces as grass, dirt and cement. Indoor training usually means training your dog to newspaper.

When deciding on the surface and location that you will want your Staffordshire to use, be sure it is going to be permanent. Training your dog to grass and then changing your

DID YOU KNOW?
Occasionally, a dog and owner who have not attended formal classes have been able to earn entry-level titles by obtaining competition rules and regulations from a local kennel club and practising on their own to a degree of perfection. Obtaining the higher level titles, however, almost always requires extensive training under the tutelage of experienced instructors. In addition, the more difficult levels require more specialised equipment whereas the lower levels do not.

mind two months later is extremely difficult for both dog and owner.

Next, choose the command you will use each and every time you want your puppy to void. 'Go hurry up' and 'Go make' are examples of commands commonly used by dog owners.

Get in the habit of asking the puppy, 'Do you want to go hurry up?' (or whatever your chosen relief command is) before you take him out. That way, when he becomes an adult, you will be able to determine if he wants to go out when you ask him. A confirmation will be signs of interest, wagging his tail, watching you intently, going to the door, etc.

PUPPY'S NEEDS

Puppy needs to relieve himself after play periods, after each meal, after he has been sleeping

and any time he indicates that he is looking for a place to urinate or defecate.

The urinary and intestinal tract muscles of very young puppies are not fully developed. Therefore, like human babies, puppies need to relieve themselves frequently.

Take your puppy out often—every hour for an eight-week-old, for example. The older the puppy, the less often he will need to relieve himself. Finally, as a mature healthy adult, he will require only three to five relief trips per day.

HOUSING

Since the types of housing and control you provide for your puppy has a direct relationship on the success of housetraining, we consider the various aspects of both before we begin training.

Bringing a new puppy home and turning him loose in

Staffs can be trained to relieve themselves on grass, sand, dirt, pavement or even on such hard surfaces as patio stone. The relief site depends upon your selection of the area most convenient for you.

If an owner has no other option but to teach the puppy relieve itself indoors, newspaper or another absorbent paper is the best choice.

81

If paper-training your Staff, use newspaper ONLY in the designated relief area.

your house can be compared to turning a child loose in a sports arena and telling the child that the place is all his! The sheer enormity of the place would be too much for him to handle.

Instead, offer the puppy clearly defined areas where he can play, sleep, eat and live. A room of the house where the family gathers is the most obvious choice. Puppies are social animals and need to feel a part of the pack right from the start. Hearing your voice, watching you while you are doing things and smelling you nearby are all positive reinforcers that he is now a member of your pack. Usually a family room, the kitchen or a nearby adjoining breakfast nook is ideal for providing safety and security

To a Staff, his home is his castle. Staffs must have a place they can recognise as their own. This dog house provides a safe haven for these two Staff chums while out in the garden.

for both puppy and owner.

Within that room there should be a smaller area which the puppy can call his own. A cubbyhole, a wire or fibreglass dog crate or a fenced (not boarded!) corner from which he can view the activities of his new family will be fine. The size of the area or crate is the key factor here. The area must be large enough for the puppy to lay down and stretch out as well as stand up without rubbing his head on the top, yet small enough so that he cannot relieve himself at one end and sleep at the other without coming into contact with his droppings.

Dogs are, by nature, clean animals and will not remain close to their relief areas unless forced to do so. In those cases, they then become dirty dogs and usually remain that way for life.

The crate or cubby should be lined with a clean towel and offer one toy, no more. Do not put food or water in the crate, as eating and drinking will activate his digestive processes and ultimately defeat your purpose as well as make the puppy very uncomfortable as he attempts to 'hold it.'

CONTROL
By control, we mean helping the puppy to create a lifestyle pattern that will be compatible to that of his human pack (YOU!). Just as we guide little children to learn our way

> **DID YOU KNOW?**
> Do not carry your dog to his toilet area. Lead him there on a leash or, better yet, encourage him to follow you to the spot. If you start carrying him to his spot, you might end up doing this routine forever and your dog will have the satisfaction of having trained YOU.

of life, we must show the puppy when it is time to play, eat, sleep, exercise and even entertain himself.

Your puppy should always sleep in his crate. He should also learn that, during times of household confusion and excessive human activity such as at breakfast when family members are preparing for the

Young puppies have very little control of their anatomy. Owners must take pups out every hour or two to relieve themselves.

> **DID YOU KNOW?**
> Stand up straight and authoritatively when giving your dog commands. Do not issue commands when lying on the floor or lying on your back on the sofa. If you are on your hands and knees when you give a command, your dog will think you are positioning yourself to play.

DID YOU KNOW?
Practice Makes Perfect!
• Have training lessons with your dog every day in several short segments—three to five times a day for a few minutes at a time is ideal.
• Do not have long practice sessions. The dog will become easily bored.
• Never practice when you are tired, ill, worried or in an otherwise negative mood. This will transmit to the dog and may have an adverse effect on its performance.
Think fun, short and above all POSITIVE! End each session on a high note, rather than a failed exercise, and make sure to give a lot of praise. Enjoy the training and help your dog enjoy it, too.

chair and is incapable of making the association of the discipline with his naughty deed.)

Other times of excitement, such as family parties, etc., can be fun for the puppy providing he can view the activities from the security of his crate. He is not underfoot and he is not being fed all sorts of titbits that will probably cause him stomach distress, yet he still feels a part of the fun.

SCHEDULE
As stated earlier, a puppy should be taken to his relief area each time he is released from his crate, after meals, after a play session, when he first awakens in the morning (at age 8 weeks, this can mean 5 a.m.!) and whenever he indicates by circling or sniffing busily that

day, he can play by himself in relative safety and comfort in his crate. Each time you leave the puppy alone, he should be crated. Puppies are chewers. They cannot tell the difference between lamp cords, television wires, shoes, table legs, etc. Chewing into a television wire, for example, can be fatal to the puppy while a shorted wire can start a fire in the house.

If the puppy chews on the arm of the chair when he is alone, you will probably discipline him angrily when you get home. Thus, he makes the association that your coming home means he is going to be hit or punished. (He will not remember chewing up the

DID YOU KNOW?
By providing sleeping and resting quarters that fit the dog, and offering frequent opportunities to relieve himself outside his quarters, the puppy quickly learns that the outdoors (or the newspaper if you are training him to paper) is the place to go when he needs to urinate or defecate. It also reinforces his innate desire to keep his sleeping quarters clean. This, in turn, helps develop the muscle control that will eventually produce a dog with clean living habits.

he needs to urinate or defecate. For a puppy less than ten weeks of age, a routine of taking him out every hour is necessary. As the puppy grows, he will be able to wait for longer periods of time.

Keep trips to his relief area short. Stay no more than five or six minutes and then return to the house. If he goes during that time, praise him lavishly and take him indoors immediately. If he does not, but he has an accident when you go back indoors, pick him up immediately, say 'No! No!' and return to his relief area. Wait a few minutes, then return to the house again. NEVER hit a puppy or rub his face in urine or excrement when he has an accident!

Once indoors, put the puppy in his crate until you have had time to clean up his

A durable fibreglass crate is ideal for travelling for your Staff, though wire crates are preferred for everyday use in the home.

accident. Then release him to the family area and watch him more closely than before. Chances are, his accident was a result of your not picking up his signal or waiting too long before offering him the opportunity to relieve himself. NEVER hold a grudge against the puppy for accidents.

Let the puppy learn that going outdoors means it is time to relieve himself, not play. Once trained, he will be able to play indoors and out and still differentiate between the times for play versus the times for relief.

Help him develop regular hours for naps, being alone, playing by himself and just resting, all in his crate. Encourage him to entertain himself while you are busy with your activities. Let him learn that having you near is

DID YOU KNOW?

Success that comes by luck is usually happenstance and frequently short lived. Success that comes by well-thought-out proven methods is often more easily achieved and permanent. This is the Success Method. It is designed to give you, the puppy owner, a simple yet proven way to help yourStaffordshire puppy develop clean living habits and a feeling of security in his new environment.

Every dog must be crate trained.

House training males is more difficult than females. Male Staffs mark their territory on trees, bushes, and any other vertical object that captures their fancy, such as this one!

comforting, but it is not your main purpose in life to provide him with undivided attention.

Each time you put a puppy in his crate tell him, 'Crate time!' (or whatever command you choose). Soon, he will run to his crate when he hears you say those words.

In the beginning of his training, do not leave him in his crate for prolonged periods of time except during the night when everyone is sleeping. Make his experience with his crate a pleasant one and, as an adult, he will love his crate and

willingly stay in it for several hours. There are millions of people who go to work every day and leave their adult dogs crated while they are away. The dogs accept this as their lifestyle and look forward to 'crate time.'

Crate training provides safety for you, the puppy and the home. It also provides the puppy with a feeling of security, and that helps the puppy achieve self-confidence and clean habits.

Remember that one of the primary ingredients in housetraining your puppy is control. Regardless of your lifestyle, there will always be occasions when you will need to have a place where your dog can stay and be happy and safe. Crate training is the answer for now and in the future.

In conclusion, a few key elements are really all you need

Your Staff should have a crate large enough for him to stand erect. It should be sturdy and strong enough to support moderate weights, too.

Canine Development Schedule

It is important to understand how and at what age a puppy develops into adulthood. If you are a puppy owner, consult the following Canine Development Schedule to determine the stage of development your Staffordshire Bull Terrier puppy is currently experiencing. This knowledge will help you as you work with the puppy in the weeks and months ahead.

Period	Age	Characteristics
FIRST TO THIRD	**BIRTH TO SEVEN WEEKS**	Puppy needs food, sleep and warmth, and responds to simple and gentle touching. Needs mother for security and disciplining. Needs litter mates for learning and interacting with other dogs. Pup learns to function within a pack and learns pack order of dominance. Begin socialising with adults and children for short periods. Begins to become aware of its environment.
FOURTH	**EIGHT TO TWELVE WEEKS**	Brain is fully developed. Needs socialising with outside world. Remove from mother and littermates. Needs to change from canine pack to human pack. Human dominance necessary. Fear period occurs between 8 and 16 weeks. Avoid fright and pain.
FIFTH	**THIRTEEN TO SIXTEEN WEEKS**	Training and formal obedience should begin. Less association with other dogs, more with people, places, situations. Period will pass easily if you remember this is pup's change-to-adolescence time. Be firm and fair. Flight instinct prominent. Permissiveness and over-disciplining can do permanent damage. Praise for good behaviour.
JUVENILE	**FOUR TO EIGHT MONTHS**	Another fear period about 7 to 8 months of age. It passes quickly, but be cautious of fright and pain. Sexual maturity reached. Dominant traits established. Dog should understand sit, down, come and stay by now.

NOTE: THESE ARE APPROXIMATE TIME FRAMES. ALLOW FOR INDIVIDUAL DIFFERENCES IN PUPPIES.

for a successful house and crate training method—consistency, frequency, praise, control and supervision. By following these procedures with a normal, healthy puppy, you and the puppy will soon be past the stage of 'accidents' and ready to move on to a full and rewarding life together.

ROLES OF DISCIPLINE, REWARD AND PUNISHMENT

Discipline, training one to act in accordance with rules, brings order to life. It is as simple as that. Without discipline, particularly in a group society, chaos reigns supreme and the group will eventually perish. Humans and canines are social animals and need some form of discipline in order to function effectively. They must procure food, protect their home base and their young and reproduce

to keep the species going.

If there were no discipline in the lives of social animals, they would eventually die from starvation and/or predation by other stronger animals.

In the case of domestic canines, dogs need discipline in their lives in order to understand how their pack (you and other family members) function and how they must act in order to survive.

A large humane society in a highly populated area recently surveyed dog owners regarding their satisfaction with their relationships with their dogs. People who had trained their dogs were 75% more satisfied with their pets than those who had never trained their dogs.

Dr. Edward Thorndike, a psychologist, established *Thorndike's Theory of Learning*, which states that a behaviour that results in a pleasant event tends to be repeated. A behaviour that results in an unpleasant event tends not to be repeated. It is this theory on which training methods are based today. For example, if you manipulate a dog to perform a specific behaviour and reward him for doing it, he is likely to do it again because he enjoyed the end result.

Occasionally, punishment, a penalty inflicted for an offence, is necessary. The best type of punishment often comes from an outside source. For example, a child is told not to touch the stove because he may get burned. He disobeys and touches the stove. In doing so, he receives a burn. From that time on, he respects the heat of the stove and avoids contact with it. Therefore, a behaviour that results in an unpleasant event tends not to be repeated.

A good example of a dog learning the hard way is the dog who chases the house cat. He is told many times to leave the cat alone, yet he persists in teasing the cat. Then, one day he begins

> **DID YOU KNOW?**
> If you want to be successful in training your dog, you have four rules to obey yourself:
> 1. Develop an understanding of how a dog thinks.
> 2. Do not blame the dog for lack of communication.
> 3. Define your dog's personality and act accordingly.
> 4. Have patience and be consistent.

chasing the cat but the cat turns and swipes a claw across the dog's face, leaving him with a painful gash on his nose. The final result is that the dog stops chasing the cat.

TRAINING EQUIPMENT
COLLAR
A simple buckle collar is fine for most dogs. One who pulls mightily on the leash may require a chain choker collar. Only in the most severe cases of a dog being totally out of control is the use of a prong or pinch collar recomended and, only if the owner has been instructed in the proper use of such equipment. In some areas, such as the United Kingdom, these types of collars are not allowed.

LEAD
A 1- to 2-metre lead is recommended, preferably made of leather, nylon or heavy cloth. A chain lead is not

> **DID YOU KNOW?**
> The golden rule of dog training is simple. For each 'question' (command), there is only one correct answer (reaction). One command = one reaction. Keep practising the command until the dog reacts correctly without hesitating. Be repetitive but not monotonous. Dogs get bored just as people do!

The BUCKLE or LEATHER COLLAR is the standard collar used for every day purpose. Be sure that you adjust the buckle on growing puppies. Check it every day. It can become too tight overnight! These collars can be made of leather or nylon. Attach your dog's identification tags to this collar.

The CHOKE CHAIN is the usual collar recommended for training. It is constructed of highly polished steel so that it slides easily through the stainless steel loop. The idea is that the dog controls the pressure around its neck and he will stop pulling if the collar becomes uncomfortable. Never leave a choke collar on your dog when not training.

The HALTER is for a trained dog that has to be restrained to prevent running away, chasing a cat and the like. Considered the most humane of all collars, it is frequently used on smaller dogs for which collars are not comfortable.

recommended, as many dog owners find that the chain cuts into their hands and that frequently switching the lead back and forth between their hands is painful.

TREATS
Have a bag of treats on hand. Something nutritious and easy to swallow works best. Use a soft treat, a chunk of cheese or a piece of cooked chicken rather than a dry biscuit. By the time the dog gets done chewing a dry treat, he will forget why he is being rewarded in the first place! Using food rewards will not teach a dog to beg at the table—the only way to teach a dog to beg at the table is to give him food from the table. In training, rewarding the dog with a food treat will help him associate praise and the treats with learning new behaviours that obviously please his owner.

TRAINING BEGINS: ASK THE DOG A QUESTION
In order to teach your dog anything, you must first get his attention. After all, he cannot learn anything if he is looking away from you with his mind on something else.

To get his attention, ask him, 'School?' and immediately walk over to him and give him a treat as you tell him 'Good dog.' Wait a minute or two and repeat the routine, this time with a treat in your hand as you approach within a foot of the dog. Do not go directly to him, but stop about a foot short of him and hold out the treat as you ask, 'School?' He will see you approaching with a treat in your hand and most likely begin walking toward you. As you meet, give him the treat and praise again.

The third time, ask the question, have a treat in your hand and walk only a short distance toward the dog so that he must walk almost all the way to you. As he reaches you, give him the treat and praise again.

By this time, the dog will probably be getting the idea that if he pays attention to you, especially when you ask that question, it will pay off in treats and fun activities for him. In other words, he learns that 'school' means doing fun things with you that result in treats and positive attention for him.

Remember that the dog does not understand your verbal language, he only recognises

Never underestimate the power of food over a dog. Make your Staffordshire sit and stay before presenting him with his evening meal. This structure and discipline sets the tone of your leadership role.

sounds. Your question translates to a series of sounds for him, and those sounds become the signal to go to you and pay attention; if he does, he will get to interact with you plus receive treats and praise.

THE BASIC COMMANDS
TEACHING SIT
Now that you have the dog's attention, attach his lead and hold it in your left hand and a food treat in your right. Place your food hand at the dog's nose and let him lick the treat but not take it from you. Say 'Sit' and slowly raise your food hand from in front of the dog's nose up over his head so that he is looking at the ceiling. As

> ### DID YOU KNOW?
> Dogs are as different from each other as people are. What works for one dog may not work for another. Have an open mind. If one method of training is unsuccessful, try another.

he bends his head upward, he will have to bend his knees to maintain his balance. As he bends his knees, he will assume a sit position. At that point, release the food treat and praise lavishly with comments such as 'Good dog! Good sit!', etc. Remember to always praise enthusiastically, because dogs relish verbal praise from their owners and feel so proud of themselves whenever they accomplish a behaviour.

You will not use food forever in getting the dog to obey your commands. Food is only used to teach new behaviours, and once the dog knows what you want when you give a specific command, you will wean him off of the food treats but still maintain the verbal praise. After all, you will always have your voice with you, and there will be many times when you have no food rewards but expect the dog to obey.

TEACHING DOWN

Teaching the down exercise is easy when you understand how the dog perceives the down position, and it is very difficult when you do not. Dogs perceive the down position as a submissive one. Therefore, teaching the down exercise using a forceful method can sometimes make the dog develop such a fear of the down that he either runs away when you say 'down' or he attempts to bite the person who tries to force him down.

Have the dog sit close alongside your left leg, facing in the same direction as you are. Hold the lead in your left hand and a food treat in your right. Now place your left hand lightly on the top of the dog's shoulders where they meet above the spinal cord. Do not push down on the dog's shoulders; simply rest your left hand there so you can guide the dog to lie down close to your left leg rather than to

All dogs should always have a light buckle collar to which their identification is attached. Instruct your children never to remove these easily detached collars. We promised little Jaime to mention her name if she posed with her Staff Little Bug.

swing away from your side when he drops.

Now place the food hand at the dog's nose, say 'Down' very softly (almost a whisper), and slowly lower the food hand to the dog's front feet. When the food hand reaches the floor, begin moving it forward along the floor in front of the dog. Keep talking softly to the dog, saying things like, 'Do you want this treat? You can do this, good dog.' Your reassuring tone of voice will help calm the dog as he tries to follow the food hand in order to get the treat.

When the dog's elbows touch the floor, release the food and praise softly. Try to get the dog to maintain that down position for several seconds before you let him sit up again. The goal here is to get the dog to settle down and not feel threatened in the down position.

TEACHING STAY

It is easy to teach the dog to stay in either a sit or a down position. Again, we use food and praise during the teaching process as we help the dog to understand exactly what it is that we are expecting him to do.

To teach the sit/stay, start with the dog sitting on your left side as before and hold the lead in your left hand. Have a food

93

Treats are excellent motivation for dog training exercises. Pet shops sell a variety of dog treats, or small pieces of cheese will usually suffice.

treat in your right hand and place your food hand at the dog's nose. Say 'Stay' and step out on your right foot to stand directly in front of the dog, toe to toe, as he licks and nibbles the treat. Be sure to keep his head facing upward to maintain the sit position. Count to five and then swing around to stand next to the dog again with him on your left. As soon as you get back to the original position, release the food and praise lavishly.

To teach the down/stay, do the down as previously described. As soon as the dog lies down, say 'Stay' and step out on your right foot just as you did in the sit/stay. Count to five and then return to stand beside the dog with him on your left side. Release the treat and praise as always.

Within a week or ten days, you can begin to add a bit of distance between you and your dog when you leave him. When you do, use your left hand open

with the palm facing the dog as a stay signal, much the same as the hand signal a police officer uses to stop traffic at an intersection. Hold the food treat in your right hand as before, but this time the food is not touching the dog's nose. He will watch the food hand and quickly learn that he is going to get that treat as soon as you return to his side.

When you can stand 1 metre away from your dog for 30 seconds, you can then begin building time and distance in both stays. Eventually, the dog can be expected to remain in the stay position for prolonged periods of time until you return to him or call him to you. Always praise lavishly when he stays.

TEACHING COME
If you make teaching 'Come' a fun experience, you should

DID YOU KNOW?
Dogs will do anything for your attention. If you reward the dog when he is calm and resting, you will develop a well-mannered dog. If, on the other hand, you greet your dog excitedly and encourage him to wrestle and roughhouse with you, the dog will greet you the same way and you will have a hyper dog on your hands.

never have a 'student' that does not love the game or that fails to come when called. The secret, it seems, is never to teach the word 'Come.'

At times when an owner most wants his dog to come when called, the owner is likely upset or anxious and he

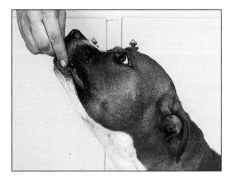

allows these feelings to come through in the tone of his voice when he calls his dog. Hearing that desperation in his owner's voice, the dog fears the results of going to him and therefore either disobeys outright or runs in the opposite direction. The secret, therefore, is to teach the dog a game and, when you want him to come to you, simply play the game. It is practically a no-fail solution!

To begin, have several members of your family take a few food treats and each go into a different room in the house. Take turns calling the dog, and each person should celebrate

the dog's finding him with a treat and lots of happy praise. When a person calls the dog, he is actually inviting the dog to find him and get a treat as a reward for 'winning.'

A few turns of the 'Where are you?' game and the dog will figure out that everyone is playing the game and that each person has a big celebration awaiting his success at locating them. Once he learns to love the game, simply calling out 'Where are you?' will bring him running from wherever he is when he hears that all-important question.

The come command is

Reward your Staff with a taste of the treat whilst you are training. Remember that there's a difference between a treat and a meal.

DID YOU KNOW?

If your dog gets lost, he is not able to ask for directions home.

Identification tags fastened to the collar give important information—the dog's name, the owner's name, the owner's address and a telephone number where the owner can be reached. This makes it easy for whoever finds the dog to contact the owner and arrange to have the dog returned. An added advantage is that a person will be more likely to approach a lost dog who has ID tags on his collar; it tells the person that this is somebody's pet rather than a stray. This is the easiest and fastest method of identification provided that the tags stay on the collar and the collar stays on the dog.

recognised as one of the most important things to teach a dog, but there are trainers who work with thousands of dogs and never teach the actual word 'Come.' Yet these dogs will race to respond to a person who

Your Staffordshire should wear his collar with ID tags at all times

uses the dog's name followed by 'Where are you?' For example, a woman has a 12-year-old companion dog who went blind, but who never fails to locate her owner when asked, 'Where are you?'

Children particularly love to play this game with their dogs. Children can hide in smaller places like a shower or bathtub, behind a bed or under a table. The dog needs to work a little bit harder to find these hiding places, but when he does he loves to celebrate with a treat and a tussle with a favourite youngster.

TEACHING HEEL

Heeling means that the dog walks beside the owner without pulling. It takes time and patience on the owner's part to succeed at teaching the dog that he (the owner) will not proceed unless the dog is walking

calmly beside him. Pulling out ahead on the lead is definitely not acceptable.

Begin with holding the lead in your left hand as the dog sits beside your left leg. Move the loop end of the lead to your right hand but keep your left hand short on the lead so it keeps the dog in close to you.

Say 'Heel' and step forward on your left foot. Keep the dog close to you and take three steps. Stop and have the dog sit next to you in what we now call the 'heel position.' Praise verbally, but do not touch the dog. Hesitate a moment and begin again with 'Heel,' taking three steps and stopping, at which point the dog is told to sit again.

Your goal here is to have the dog walk those three steps without pulling on the lead. When he will walk calmly beside you for three steps without pulling, increase the number of steps you take to

DID YOU KNOW?

When calling the dog, do not say 'Come.' Say things like, 'Rover, where are you? See if you can find me! I have a cookie for you!' Keep up a constant line of chatter with coaxing sounds and frequent questions such as, 'Where are you?' The dog will learn to follow the sound of your voice to locate you and receive his reward.

Staffs are very active and can be taught many everyday chores, but they can also enjoy a backpacking holiday in the hills.

five. When he will walk politely beside you while you take five steps, you can increase the length of your walk to ten steps. Keep increasing the length of your stroll until the dog will walk quietly beside you without pulling as long as you want him to heel. When you stop heeling, indicate to the dog that the exercise is over by verbally praising as you pet him and say 'OK, good dog.' The 'OK' is used as a release word meaning that the exercise is finished and the dog is free to relax.

If you are dealing with a dog who insists on pulling you around, simply 'put on your brakes' and stand your ground until the dog realises that the two of you are not going anywhere until he is beside you and moving at your pace, not his. It may take some time just standing there to convince the dog that you are the leader and you will be the one to decide

DID YOU KNOW?

If you begin teaching the heel by taking long walks and letting the dog pull you along, he misinterprets this action as an acceptable form of taking a walk. When you pull back on the lead to counteract his pulling, he reads that tug as a signal to pull even harder!

> **DID YOU KNOW?**
>
> Teach your dog to HEEL in an enclosed area. Once you think the dog will obey reliably and you want to attempt advanced obedience exercises such as off-lead heeling, test him in a fenced in area so he cannot run away.

on the direction and speed of your travel.

Each time the dog looks up at you or slows down to give a slack lead between the two of you, quietly praise him and say, 'Good heel. Good dog.' Eventually, the dog will begin to respond and within a few days he will be walking polite-ly beside you without pulling on the lead. At first, the training sessions should be kept short and very positive; soon the dog will be able to walk nicely with you for increasingly longer distances. Remember also to give the dog free time and the opportunity to run and play when you are done with heel practice.

WEANING OFF FOOD IN TRAINING

Food is used in training new behaviours. Once the dog understands what behaviour goes with a specific command, it is time to start weaning him off the food treats. At first, give a treat after each exercise. Then, start to give a treat only after every other exercise. Mix up the times when you offer a food reward and the times when you only offer praise so that the dog will never know when he is going to receive both food and praise and when he is going to receive only praise. This is called a variable ratio reward system and it proves successful because there is always the chance that the owner will produce a treat, so the dog never stops trying for that reward. No matter what, ALWAYS give verbal praise.

OBEDIENCE CLASSES

As previously discussed, it is a good idea to enroll in an obedience class if one is available in your area.

Training a dog to accept bribes for the successful execution of commands is simple. Weaning them off food bribes is more difficult.

Many areas have dog clubs that offer basic obedience training as well as preparatory classes for obedience competition. There are also local dog trainers who offer similar classes.

At obedience trials, dogs can earn titles at various levels of competition. The beginning levels of competition include basic behaviours such as sit, down, heel, etc. The more advanced levels of competition include jumping, retrieving, scent discrimination and signal work. The advanced levels require a dog and owner to put a lot of time and effort into their training, and the titles that can be earned at these levels of competition are very prestigious.

OTHER ACTIVITIES FOR LIFE
Whether a dog is trained in the structured environment of a class or alone with his owner at

DID YOU KNOW?
A dog in jeopardy never lies down. He stays alert on his feet because instinct tells him that he may have to run away or fight for his survival. Therefore, if a dog feels threatened or anxious, he will not lie down. Consequently, it is important to have the dog calm and relaxed as he learns the down exercise.

home, there are many activities that can bring fun and rewards to both owner and dog once they have mastered basic control.

Teaching the dog to help out around the home, in the garden or on the farm provides great satisfaction to both dog and owner. In addition, the dog's help makes life a little easier for his owner and raises his stature as a valued companion to his family. It helps give the dog a purpose by occupying

Enrolling your Staffordshire in an obedience class may be the best choice you can make in training your dog. When properly instructed, Staffs can shine in every area of obedience.

99

Can you believe that a Staffordshire Bull Terrier in good physical condition can jump as high as a man? Staffs enjoy the challenge of intense physical training.

his mind and providing an outlet for his energy.

Backpacking is an exciting and healthful activity that the dog can be taught without assistance from more than his owner. The exercise of walking and climbing is good for man and dog alike, and the bond that they develop together is priceless.

If you are interested in participating in organised competition with your Staffordshire, there are activities other than obedience in which you and your dog can become involved. Agility is a popular and fun sport where dogs run through an obstacle course that includes various jumps, tunnels and other exercises to test the dog's speed and coordination. The owners often run through the course beside their dogs to give

100

commands and to guide them through the course. Although competitive, the focus is on fun—it's fun to do, fun to watch, and great exercise.

As a Staffordshire owner, you have the opportunity to participate in Schutzhund competition if you choose. Schutzhund originated as a test to determine the best quality dogs to be used for breeding stock. Breeders continue to use it as a way to evaluate working ability and temperament. There are three levels in Schutzhund trials: SchH. I, SchH. II and

SchH. III, with each level being progressively more difficult to complete successfully. Each level consists of training, obedience and protection phases. Training for Schutzhund is intense and must be practised consistently to keep the dog keen. The experience of Schutzhund training is very rewarding for dog and owner, and the Staffordshire's tractability is well suited for this type of training.

THE SUCCESS METHOD
6 Steps to Successful Crate Training

1 Tell the puppy 'Crate time!' and place him in the crate with a small treat (a piece of cheese or half of a biscuit). Let him stay in the crate for five minutes while you are in the same room. Then release him and praise lavishly. Never release him when he is fussing. Wait until he is quiet before you let him out.

2 Repeat Step 1 several times a day.

3 The next day, place the puppy in the crate as before. Let him stay there for ten minutes. Do this several times.

4 Continue building time in five-minute increments until the puppy

stays in his crate for 30 minutes with you in the room. Always take him to his relief area after prolonged periods in his crate.

5 Now go back to Step 1 and let the puppy stay in his crate for five minutes, this time while you are out of the room.

6 Once again, build crate time in five-minute increments with you out of the room. When the puppy will stay willingly in his crate (he may even fall asleep!) for 30 minutes with you out of the room, he will be ready to stay in it for several hours at a time.

MEDICAL PROBLEMS SEEN IN STAFFORDSHIRE BULL TERRIERS

Condition	Age Affected	Cause	Area Affected
Acral Lick Dermatitis	Any age, males	Unknown	Legs
Bilateral Cataracts	Younger dogs	Congenital	Eye
Cleft Palate/Harelip	Newborns	Congenital	Hard or soft palate
Elbow Dysplasia	4 to 7 mos.	Congenital	Elbow joint
Gastric Dilatation (Bloat)	Older dogs	Swallowing air	Stomach
Hip Dysplasia	4 to 9 mos.	Congenital	Hip joint
Patellar Luxation	Any age	Congenital or acquired	Kneecaps
Progressive Retinal Atrophy	Older dogs	Congenital	Retina
Urolithiasis	Adult	Cystine uroliths/stones	Kidney/Bladder
Von Willebrand's Disease	Birth	Congenital	Blood

HEALTH CARE OF YOUR
Staffordshire Bull Terrier

Dogs suffer many of the same physical illnesses as people. They might even share many of the psychological problems. Since people usually know more about human diseases than canine maladies, many of the terms used in this chapter will be familiar, but not necessarily those used by veterinary surgeons. We'll use the term X-RAY, instead of the more acceptable term RADIOGRAPH. We will also use the familiar term SYMPTOMS even though dogs don't have symptoms, which are are verbal descriptions of the patient's feelings. Since dogs can't speak, we have to look for clinical signs...but we still use the term SYMPTOMS in this book.

As a general rule, medicine is PRACTISED. That term is not arbitrary. Medicine is a constantly changing art as we learn more and more about genetics, electronic aids (like CAT scans) and opinions. There are many dog maladies, like canine hip dysplasia, which are not universally treated in the same manner. Some veterinary surgeons opt for surgery more often than others.

SELECTING A VETERINARY SURGEON

Your selection of a veterinary surgeon should not be based upon personality (as most are) but upon their convenience to your home. You want a doctor who is close as you might have emergencies or multiple visits for treatments. You want a doctor who has services that you might require such as a boarding kennel and grooming facilities, as well as sophisticated pet supplies and a good reputation for ability and responsiveness. There is nothing more frustrating than having to wait a day or more to get a response from a veterinary surgeon.

All veterinary surgeons are licensed and their diplomas and/or certificates should be

Veterinary surgeon examining an x-ray. You should choose a vet before bringing your Staffordshire puppy home.

103

displayed in their waiting rooms. There are, however, many veterinary specialties which usually require further studies and internships. There are specialists in heart problems (veterinary cardiologists), skin problems

Your veterinary surgeon will be your dog's friend throughout his life.

(veterinary dermatologists), teeth and gum problems (veterinary dentists), eye problems (veterinary ophthalmologists), X-rays (veterinary radiologists), and surgeons who have specialties in bones, muscles or other organs. Most veterinary surgeons do routine surgery such as neutering, stitching up wounds and docking tails for those breeds in which such is required for show purposes. When the problem affecting your dog is serious, it is not unusual or impudent to get another medical opinion. You might also want to compare costs among several veterinary surgeons. Sophisticated health care and veterinary services can be very costly. Don't be bashful about discussing these costs with your veterinary surgeon or his (her) staff. It is not infrequent that important decisions are based upon financial considerations.

PREVENTATIVE MEDICINE
It is much easier, less costly and more effective to practise preventative medicine than to fight bouts of illness and disease.

Properly bred puppies come from parents that were selected based upon their genetic disease profile. Their mothers should have been vaccinated, free of all internal and external parasites, and properly nourished. For these reasons, a visit to the veterinary surgeon who cared for the dam (mother) is recommended. The dam can pass on disease resistance to her puppies, which can last for eight to ten weeks. She can also pass on parasites and many infections. That's why you should visit the veterinary surgeon who cared for the dam.

WEANING TO FIVE MONTHS OLD
Puppies should be weaned by the time they are about two months old. A puppy that remains for at least eight weeks with its mother and litter mates

DID YOU KNOW?
Your veterinary surgeon will probably recommend that your puppy be vaccinated before you take him outside. There are airborne diseases, parasite eggs in the grass and unexpected visits from other dogs that might be dangerous to your puppy's health.

Normal Staffordshire Bull Terrier Skeletal Structure

Skull, Cervical, Thoracic Vertebrae, Lumbar Vertebrae, Sacrum, Coccygeal, Pelvis, Mandible, Scapula, Humerus, Sternum, Ulna, Radius, Carpus, Metacarpus, Femur, Tibia, Fibula, Patella, Tuber Calcis, Metatarsis, Phalanges, Tarsis

usually adapts better to other dogs and people later in its life.

In every case, you should have your newly acquired puppy examined by a veterinary surgeon immediately. Vaccination programmes usually begin when the puppy is very young.

The puppy will have its teeth examined and have its skeletal conformation and general health checked prior to certification by the veterinary surgeon. Many puppies have problems with their knee caps, eye cataracts and other eye problems, heart murmurs and undescended testicles. They may also have personality problems and your veterinary surgeon might have training in temperament evaluation.

VACCINATION SCHEDULING
Most vaccinations are given by injection and should only be done by a veterinary surgeon. Both he and you should keep a

record of the date of the injection, the identification of the vaccine and the amount given. The first vaccinations should start when the puppy is 6–8 weeks of age, the second when it is 10–12 weeks of age and the third when it is 14–16 weeks of age. Vaccinations should NEVER be given without a 15-day lapse between injections. Most vaccinations immunise your puppy against viruses.

The usual vaccines contain immunising doses of several different viruses such as distemper, parvovirus, parainfluenza and hepatitis. There are other vaccines available when the puppy is at risk. You should rely upon professional advice. This is especially true for the booster shot programme. Most vaccination programmes require a booster when the puppy is a year old, and once a year thereafter. In some cases, circumstances may require more

DID YOU KNOW?

Vaccines do not work all the time. Sometimes dogs are allergic to them and many times the antibodies, which are supposed to be stimulated by the vaccine, just are not produced. You should keep your dog in the veterinary clinic for an hour after it is vaccinated to be sure there are no allergic reactions.

frequent immunisations.

Canine cough, more formally known as tracheobronchitis, is treated with a vaccine which is sprayed into the dog's nostrils.

The effectiveness of a parvovirus vaccination programme can be tested by using the parovirus antibody titer to be certain that the vaccinations are protective. Your veterinary surgeon will explain and manage all of these details.

FIVE MONTHS TO ONE YEAR OF AGE
By the time your puppy is five months old, he should have completed his vaccination programme. During his physical examination he should be evaluated for the common hip dysplasia and other diseases of the joints. There are tests to assist in the prediction of these problems. Other tests can be run to assess the effectiveness of the vaccination programme.

Unless you intend to breed or show your dog, neutering the puppy at six months of age is recommended. Discuss this with your veterinary surgeon.

By the time your Staffordshire is seven or eight months of age, he can be seriously evaluated for his conformation to the club standard, thus determining show potential and desirability as a sire or dam. If the puppy is not top class and therefore is not a candidate for a

HEALTH AND VACCINATION SCHEDULE

Age in Weeks:	3rd	6th	8th	10th	12th	14th	16th	20-24th
Worm Control	✔	✔	✔	✔	✔	✔	✔	✔
Neutering								✔
Heartworm*		✔						✔
Parvovirus		✔		✔		✔		✔
Distemper			✔		✔		✔	
Hepatitis			✔		✔		✔	
Leptospirosis		✔		✔		✔		
Parainfluenza		✔		✔		✔		
Dental Examination			✔					✔
Complete Physical			✔					✔
Temperament Testing			✔					
Coronavirus					✔			
Canine Cough		✔						
Hip Dysplasia							✔	
Rabies*								✔

Vaccinations are not instantly effective. It takes about two weeks for the dog's immunisation system to develop antibodies. Most vaccinations require annual booster shots. Your veterinary surgeon should guide you in this regard.
*Not applicable in the United Kingdom

serious breeding programme, most professionals advise neutering the puppy. Neutering has proven to be extremely beneficial to both male and female puppies. Besides eliminating the possibility of pregnancy, it inhibits (but does not prevent) breast cancer in bitches and prostate cancer in male dogs.

DOGS OLDER THAN ONE YEAR

Continue to visit the veterinary surgeon at least once a year. There is no such disease as old age, but bodily functions do change with age. The eyes and

DID YOU KNOW?

Caring for the puppy starts before the puppy is born by keeping the dam healthy and well-nourished. When the puppy is about three weeks old, it must start its disease-control regimen. The first treatments will be for worms. Most puppies have worms, even if they are tested negative for worms. The test essentially is checking the stool specimens for the eggs of the worms. The worms continually shed eggs except during their dormant stage, when they just rest in the tissues of the puppy. During this stage they don't shed eggs and are not evident during a routine examination.

ears are no longer as efficient. Liver, kidney and intestine functions often decline. Proper dietary changes, recommended by your veterinary surgeon, can make life more pleasant for the ageing Staffordshire and you.

SKIN PROBLEMS IN STAFFORDSHIRES

Veterinary surgeons are consulted by dog owners for skin problems more than any other group of diseases or maladies. Dogs' skin is almost as sensitive as human skin and both suffer almost the same ailments. (Though the occurrence of acne in dogs is rare!) For this reason, veterinary dermatology has developed into a specialty practiced by many veterinary surgeons.

Since many skin problems have visual symptoms which are almost identical, it requires the skill of an experienced veterinary dermatologist to identify and cure many of the more severe skin disorders. Pet shops sell many treatments for skin problems but most of the treatments are directed at symptoms and not the underlying problem(s). If your dog is suffering from a skin disorder, you should seek professional assistance as quickly as possible. As with all diseases, the earlier a problem is identified and treated, the more successful is the cure.

108

DID YOU KNOW?

There is a 1:4 chance of a puppy getting this fatal gene combination from two parents with recessive genes for acrodermatitis:

AA= NORMAL, HEALTHY
aa= FATAL
Aa= RECESSIVE, NORMAL APPEARING

If the female parent has an Aa gene and the male parent has an Aa gene, the chances are one in four that the puppy will have the fatal genetic combination aa.

Dam

	A	a
A	AA	Aa
a	Aa	aa

Sire

INHERITED SKIN PROBLEMS

Many skin disorders are inherited and some are fatal. For example, Acrodermatitis is an inherited disease which is transmitted by BOTH parents. The parents, which appear (phenotypically) normal, have a recessive gene for acrodermatitis, meaning that they carry, but are not affected by the disease.

Acrodermatitis is just one example of how difficult it is to prevent congenital dog diseases. The cost and skills required to ascertain whether two dogs should be mated are too high even though puppies with acrodermatitis rarely reach two years of age.

Other inherited skin problems are usually not as fatal as acrodermatitis. All inherited diseases must be diagnosed and treated by a veterinary specialist. There are active programmes being undertaken by many veterinary pharmaceutical manufacturers to solve most, if not all, of the common skin problems of dogs.

PARASITE BITES

Many of us are allergic to mosquito bites. The bites itch, erupt and may even become infected. Dogs have the same reaction to fleas, ticks and/or mites. When you feel the prick of the mosquito as it bites you, you have a chance to kill it with your hand. Unfortunately, when our dog is bitten by a flea, tick or mite, it can only scratch it away or bite it. By the time the dog has been bitten, the parasite has done some of its damage. It may also have laid eggs to cause further problems in the near future. The itching from parasite bites is

> **DID YOU KNOW?**
> Chances are that you and your dog will have the same allergies. Your allergies are readily recognizable and usually easily treated. Your dog's allergies may be masked.

> **DID YOU KNOW?**
> A dental examination is in order when the dog is between six months and one year of age and any permanent teeth that have erupted incorrectly can be corrected. It is important to begin a brushing regimen, preferably using a two-sided brushing technique, whereby both sides of the tooth are brushed at the same time. Durable nylon and safe edible chews should be a part of your puppy's arsenal for good health, good teeth and pleasant breath. The vast majority of dogs three to four years old and older has diseases of their gums from lack of dental attention. Using the various types of dental chews can be very effective in controlling dental plaque.

By the time your dog is a year old, you should have become very comfortable with your local veterinary surgeon and have agreed on scheduled visits for booster vaccinations. Blood tests should now be taken regularly, for comparative purposes, for such variables as cholesterol and triglyceride levels, thyroid hormones, liver enzymes, blood cell counts, etc.

The eyes, ears, nose and throat should be examined regularly and annual cleaning of the teeth is a ritual. For teeth scaling, the dog must be anaesthetised.

probably due to the saliva inject-ed into the site when the parasite sucks the dog's blood.

AUTO-IMMUNE SKIN CONDITIONS

Auto-immune skin conditions are commonly referred to as being allergic to yourself, although allergies are usually inflammato-ry reactions to an outside stimulus. Auto-immune diseases cause serious damage to the tissues which are involved.

The best known auto-immune disease is lupus, which affects people as well as dogs. The symptoms are variable and may affect the kidneys, bones, blood chemistry and skin. It can be fatal to both dogs and humans, though it is not thought to be transmissi-ble. It is usually successfully treated with cortisone, prednisone or similar corticos-teroid, but extensive use of these drugs can have harmful side effects.

AIRBORNE ALLERGIES

An interesting allergy is pollen allergy. Humans have hay fever, rose fever and other fevers with which they suffer during the pollinating season. Many dogs suffer the same allergies. When the pollen count is high, dogs might suffer but do not expect them to sneeze and have runny noses like humans. Dogs react to pollen allergies the same way they react to fleas—they scratch

and bite themselves. Staffordshires are very suscepti-ble to airborne pollen allergies.

Dogs, like humans, can be tested for allergens. Discuss the testing with your veterinary dermatologist.

FOOD PROBLEMS

FOOD ALLERGIES

Dogs are allergic to many foods which are best-sellers and highly recommended by breeders and veterinary surgeons. Changing the brand of food that you buy may not eliminate the problem if the element to which the dog is allergic is contained in the new brand.

Recognising a food allergy is difficult. Humans vomit or have rashes when they eat a food to which they are allergic. Dogs neither vomit nor (usually) develop a rash. They react in the same manner as they do to an airborne or flea allergy: they itch, scratch and bite, thus making the diagnosis extremely difficult. While pollen allergies and parasite bites are usually season-al, food allergies are year-round problems.

TREATING FOOD PROBLEMS

Handling food allergies and food intolerance yourself is possible. Put your dog on a diet which it has never had. Obviously if it has never eaten this new food it can't have been allergic or intolerant of it. Start with a single ingredient which is NOT in the dog's diet at the present time. Ingredients like chopped beef or fish are common in dog's diets, so try something more exotic like ostrich, rabbit, pheasant or even just vegetables. Keep the dog on this diet (with no additives) for a month. If the symptoms of food allergy or intolerance disappear, chances are your dog has a food allergy.

Don't think that the single ingredient cured the problem. You still must find a suitable diet and ascertain which ingredient in the old diet was objectionable. This is most easily done by adding ingredients to the new

> **DID YOU KNOW?**
> Food intolerance is the inability of the dog to completely digest certain foods. Puppies which may have done very well on their mother's milk may not do well on cow's milk. The result of this food intolerance may be loose bowels, passing gas and stomach pains. These are the only obvious symptoms to food intolerance and that makes diagnosis difficult.

diet one at a time. Let the dog stay on the modified diet for a month before you add another ingredient. Eventually, you will

Disease	What is it?	What causes it?	Symptoms
Leptospirosis	Severe disease that affects the internal organs; can be spread to people.	A bacterium, which is often carried by rodents, that enters through mucous membranes and spreads quickly throughout the body.	Range from fever, vomiting and loss of appetite in less severe cases to shock, irreversible kidney damage and possibly death in most severe cases.
Rabies	Potentially deadly virus that infects warm-blooded mammals. Not seen in United Kingdom.	Bite from a carrier of the virus, mainly wild animals.	1st stage: dog exhibits change in behaviour, fear. 2nd stage: dog's behaviour becomes more aggressive. 3rd stage: loss of coordination, trouble with bodily functions.
Parvovirus	Highly contagious virus, potentially deadly.	Ingestion of the virus, which is usually spread through the faeces of infected dogs.	Most common: severe diarrhoea. Also vomiting, fatigue, lack of appetite.
Kennel cough	Contagious respiratory infection.	Combination of types of bacteria and virus. Most common: *Bordetella bronchiseptica* bacteria and parainfluenza virus.	Chronic cough.
Distemper	Disease primarily affecting respiratory and nervous system.	Virus that is related to the human measles virus.	Mild symptoms such as fever, lack of appetite and mucous secretion progress to evidence of brain damage, 'hard pad.'
Hepatitis	Virus primarily affecting the liver.	Canine adenovirus type I (CAV-1). Enters system when dog breathes in particles.	Lesser symptoms include listlessness, diarrhoea, vomiting. More severe symptoms include 'blue-eye' (clumps of virus in eye).
Coronavirus	Virus resulting in digestive problems.	Virus is spread through infected dog's faeces.	Stomach upset evidenced by lack of appetite, vomiting, diarrhoea.

DID YOU KNOW?
Your dog's protein needs are changeable. High activity level, stress, climate and other physical factors may require your dog to have more protein in his diet. Check with your veterinary surgeon.

determine the ingredient that caused the adverse reaction.

An alternative method is to carefully study the ingredients in the diet to which your dog is allergic or intolerable. Identify the main ingredient in this diet and eliminate the main ingredient by buying a different food which does not have that ingredient. Keep experimenting until the symptoms disappear after one month on the new diet.

EXTERNAL PARASITES
Of all the problems to which dogs are prone, none is more well known and frustrating than fleas. Fleas, which usually refers to fleas, ticks and mites, are difficult to prevent but relatively simple to cure. Parasites that are harboured inside the body are more difficult to

DID YOU KNOW?
Feeding your dog properly is very important. An incorrect diet could affect the dog's health, behaviour and nervous system, possibly making a normal dog into an aggressive one.

cure but they are easier to control.

FLEAS
To control a flea infestation you have to understand the life cycle of a typical flea. Fleas are basically a summertime problem and their effective treatment (destruc-

DID YOU KNOW?
The myth that dogs need extra fat in their diets can be harmful. Should your vet recommend extra fat, use safflower oil instead of animal oils. Safflower oil has been shown to be less likely to cause allergic reactions.

tion) is environmental. There is no single flea-control medicine (insecticide) which can be used in every flea infested area. To understand flea control you must apply suitable treatment to the weak link in the life cycle of the flea.

THE LIFE CYCLE OF A FLEA
Fleas are found in four forms: eggs, larvae, pupae and adults. You really need a low-power microscope or hand lens to identify a living flea's eggs, pupae or larva. They spend their whole lives on your Staffordshire unless they are forcibly removed by brushing, bathing, scratching or biting.

The Life Cycle of the Flea

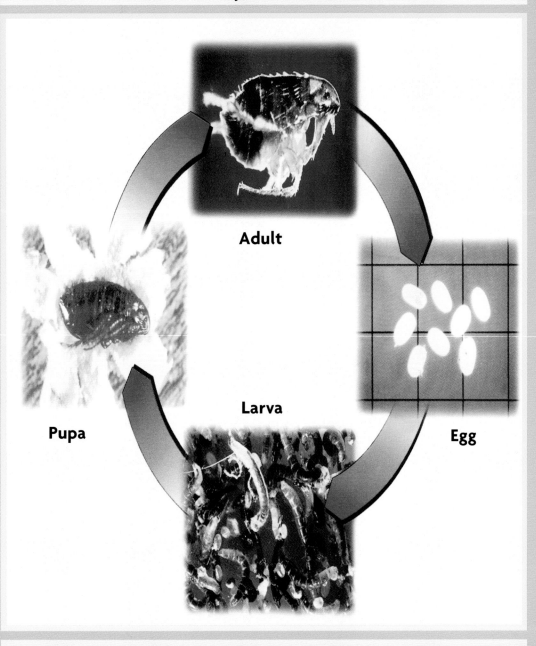

Adult

Pupa

Larva

Egg

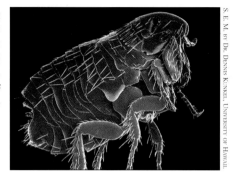

A scanning electron micrograph (S. E. M.) of a dog flea, *Ctenocephalides canis.*

S. E. M. BY DR. DENNIS KUNKEL, UNIVERSITY OF HAWAII

The dog flea is scientifically known as *Ctenocephalides canis* while the cat flea is *Ctenocephalides felis.* Several species infest both dog and cats.

Fleas lay eggs while they are in residence on your dog. These eggs fall off almost as soon as they dry (they may be a bit damp when initially laid) and are the reservoir of future flea infestations. If your dog scratches himself and is able to dislodge a few fleas, they simply fall off and await a future chance to attack a dog...or even a person. Yes, fleas from dogs bite people. That's why it is so important to control fleas both on the dog and in the dog's entire environment. You must, therefore, treat the dog and the environment simultaneously.

DE-FLEAING THE HOME
Cleanliness is the simple rule. If you have a cat living with your dog, the matter is more complicated since most dog fleas are actually cat fleas. Cats climb onto many areas that are never accessible to dogs (like window sills, table tops, etc.), so you have to clean all of these areas. The hard floor surfaces (tiles, wood, stone and linoleum) must be mopped several times a day. Drops of food onto the floor are actually food for flea larvae! All rugs and furniture must be vacuumed several times a day. Don't forget closets, under furniture and cushions. A study has reported that a vacuum cleaner with a beater bar can remove only 20% of the larvae and 50% of the eggs. The vacuum bags should be discarded into a sealed plastic bag or burned. The vacuum machine itself

DID YOU KNOW?
Fleas have been around for millions of years and have adapted to changing host animals.

They are able to go through a complete life cycle in less than one month or they can extend their lives to almost two years by remaining as pupae or cocoons. They do not need blood or any other food for up to 20 months.

They have been measured as being able to jump 300,000 times and can jump 150 times their length in any direction including straight up. Those are just a few of the reasons they are so successful in infesting a dog!

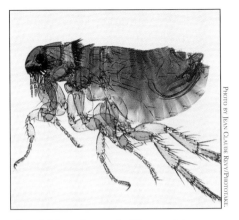

Photo by Jean Claude Revy/Phototake.

DID YOU KNOW?

There are many parasiticides which can be used around your home and garden to control fleas.

Natural pyrethrins can be used inside the house.

Allethrin, bioallethrin, permethrin and resmethrin can also be used inside the house but permethrin has been used success-fully outdoors, too.

Carbaryl can be used indoors and outdoors.

Propoxur can be used indoors.

Chlorpyrifos, diazinon and malathion can be used indoors or outdoors and it has an extended residual activity.

A male dog flea, *Ctenocephalides canis.*

should be cleaned. The outdoor area to which your dog has access must also be treated with an insecticide.

There are many drugs available to kill fleas on the dog itself, such as the miracle drug ivermectin, and it is best to have the de-fleaing and de-worming supervised by your vet. Ivermectin is effective against many external and internal parasites including heartworms, roundworms, tapeworms, flukes, ticks and mites. It has not been

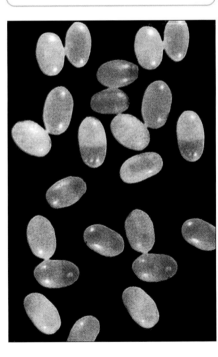

The eggs of the dog flea.

Male cat fleas, *Ctenocephalides felis*, are very commonly found on dogs.

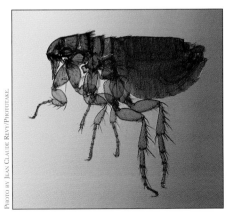

Photo by Jean Claude Revy/Phototake.

Dwight R. Kuhn's magnificent action photo showing a flea jumping from a dog's back.

PHOTO BY DWIGHT R. KUHN

(Facing Page) A scanning electron micrograph of a dog or cat flea, *Ctenocephalides*, magnified more than 100X. This has been coloured for effect.

approved for use to control these pests, but veterinary surgeons frequently use it anyway. Ivermectin may not be available in all areas.

Dogs pick up fleas outdoors, too.

STERILISING THE ENVIRONMENT

Magnified head of a dog flea, *Ctenocephalides canis*.

Besides cleaning your home with vacuum cleaners and mops, you have to treat the outdoor range of your dog. When trimming bushes and spreading insecticide, be careful not to poison areas in which fishes or other animals reside.

TICKS AND MITES

Though not as common as fleas, ticks and mites are found all over the tropical and temperate world. They don't bite like fleas, they harpoon. They dig their sharp proboscis (nose) into the dog's skin and drink the blood, which is their only food and drink. Dogs can get Lyme disease, Rocky Mountain spotted fever (normally found in the U.S.A. only), paralysis and many other diseases from ticks and mites. They may live where fleas are found but they

S. E. M. BY DR. DENNIS KUNKEL, UNIVERSITY OF HAWAII.

S. E. M. BY DR. DENNIS KUNKEL, UNIVERSITY OF HAWAII.

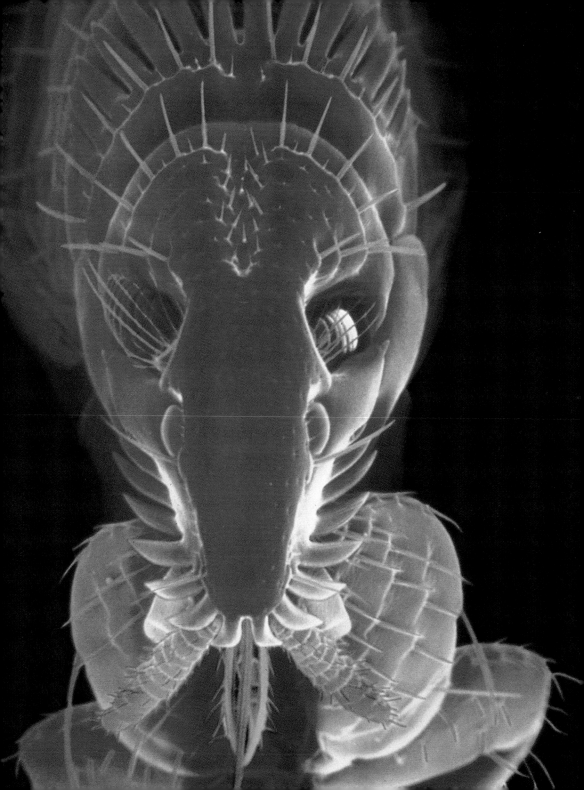

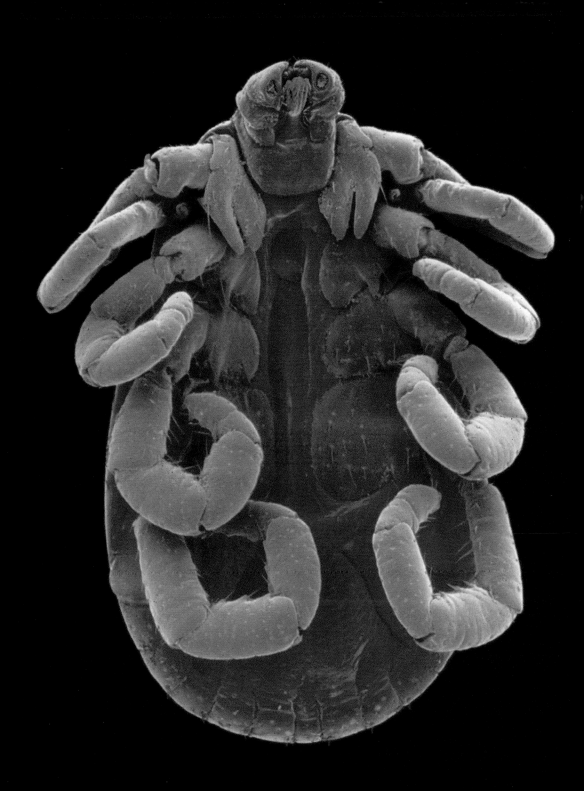

PHOTO BY DWIGHT R. KUHN

MANGE

Mange is a skin irritation caused by mites. Some mites are contagious, like *Cheyletiella*, ear mites, scabies and chiggers. The

Human lice look like dog lice; the two are closely related.

De-fleaing your dog is easy, it's ridding the surrounding environment of fleas that is difficult.

non-contagious mites are *Demodex*. The most serious of the mites is the one that causes ear mite infestation. Ear mites are usually controlled with ivermectin.

It is essential that your dog be treated for mange as quickly as possible because some forms of mange are transmissible to people.

(Facing Page) The dog tick, *Dermacentor variabilis*, is probably the most common tick found on dogs. Look at the strength in its eight legs! No wonder it's hard to detach them.

also like to hide in cracks or seams in walls wherever dogs live. They are controlled the same way fleas are controlled.

The tick *Dermacentor variabilis* may well be the most common dog tick in many geographical areas, especially where the climate is hot and humid.

Most dog ticks have life expectancies of a week to six months, depending upon climatic conditions. They neither jump nor fly, but crawl slowly and can range up to 5 metres (16 feet) to reach a sleeping or unsuspecting dog.

A brown dog tick, *Rhipicephalus sanguineus*, is an uncommon but annoying tick found on dogs.

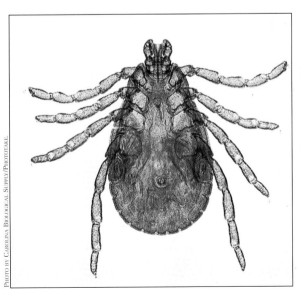

PHOTO BY CAROLINA BIOLOGICAL SUPPLY/PHOTOTAKE.

S. E. M. BY DR. DENNIS KUNKEL, UNIVERSITY OF HAWAII.

119

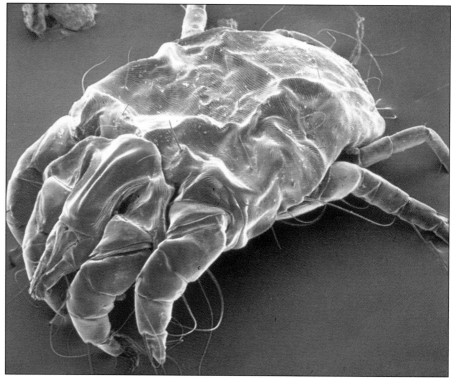

Magnified view of the mange mite, *Psoroptes bovis*.

SEM by James Hayden-Yoav/Phototake.

Acral lick syndrome results in a large open wound, a lick granuloma, usually on the dog's leg.

ACRAL LICK DISEASE

Staffordshires and other dogs about the same size have a very poorly understood syndrome called *acral lick*. The manifestation of the problem is the dog's tireless attack at a specific area of the body, almost always the legs. They lick so intensively that they remove the hair and skin leaving an ugly, large wound. There is no absolute cure, but corticosteroids are the most common treatment.

INTERNAL PARASITES

Most animals—fishes, birds and mammals, including dogs and

Simulated medical condition for educational purposes.

humans—have worms and other parasites which live inside their bodies. According to Dr. Herbert R. Axelrod, the fish pathologist, there are two kinds of parasites: dumb and smart. The smart parasites live in peaceful cooperation with their hosts (symbiosis), while the dumb parasites kill their host. Most of the worm infections are relatively easy to control. If they are not controlled they eventually weaken the host dog to the point that other medical problems occur, but they are not dumb parasites who directly cause the death of their hosts.

ROUNDWORMS

The roundworms that infect dogs are scientifically known as *Toxocara canis*. They live in the dog's intestine and shed eggs continually. It has been estimated that a Staffordshire produces about 150 grammes of faeces every day. Each gramme of faeces averages 10,000–12,000 eggs of roundworms. There are no known areas in which dogs roam that does not contain roundworm eggs. The greatest danger of roundworms is that they infect people, too! It is wise to have your dog tested regularly for roundworms.

Pigs also have roundworm infections which can be passed to human and dogs. The typical pig roundworm parasite is called *Ascaris lumbricoides*.

DID YOU KNOW?

Ivermectin is quickly becoming the drug of choice for treating many parasitic skin diseases in dogs.

For some unknown reason, herding dogs like Collies, Old English Sheepdogs and German Shepherds, etc., are extremely sensitive to ivermectin.

Ivermectin injections have killed some dogs, but dogs heavily infected with skin disorders may be treated anyway.

The ivermectin reaction is a toxicosis which causes tremors, loss of power to move their muscles, prolonged dilitation of the pupil of the eye, coma (unconsciousness), or cessation of breathing (death).

The toxicosis usually starts from 4-6 hours after ingestion (not injection), or as late as 12 hours. The longer it takes to set in, the milder is the reaction.

Ivermectin should only be prescribed and administered by a vet.

Some ivermectin treatments require two doses.

HOOKWORMS

The worm *Ancylostoma caninum* is commonly called the dog hookworm. It is also dangerous to humans and cats. It attaches itself to the intestines of the dog by its teeth. It changes the site of its attachment about six times a day, and the dog loses blood from each detachment. This blood loss can cause iron-deficiency anaemia. Hookworms are easily purged from the dog with many

DID YOU KNOW?

Average size dogs can pass 1,360,000 roundworm eggs every day.

For example, if there were only 1 million dogs in the world, the world would be saturated with 1,300 metric tonnes of dog faeces.

These faeces would contain 15,000,000,000 roundworm eggs.

7 to 31 percent of home gardens and children's play boxes in the U. S. contained roundworm eggs.

Flushing dog's faeces down the toilet is not a safe practice because the usual sewage treatments do not destroy roundworm eggs.

Infected puppies start shedding roundworm eggs at 3 weeks of age. They can be infected by their mother's milk.

medications, the best of which seems to be ivermectin even though it has not been approved for such use.

TAPEWORMS

There are many species of tapeworms. They are carried by fleas! The dog eats the flea and starts the tapeworm cycle. Humans can also be infected with tapeworms, so don't eat fleas! Fleas are so small that your dog could pass them onto your hands, your plate or your food and make it possible for you to ingest a flea which is carrying tapeworm eggs.

While tapeworm infection is not life threatening in dogs

The roundworm can infect both dogs and humans.

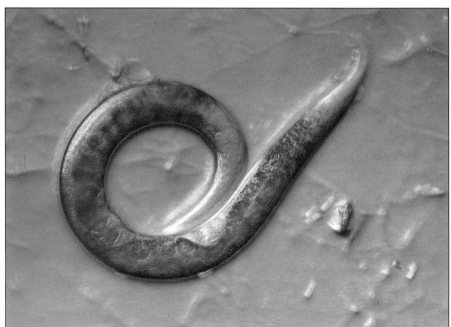

PHOTO BY DWIGHT R. KUHN.

The roundworm, *Ascaris lumbricoides*, is found in dogs, pigs and humans.

PHOTO BY DWIGHT R. KUHN.

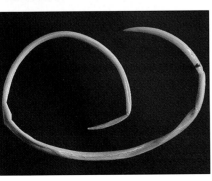

PHOTO BY CAROLINA BIOLOGICAL SUPPLY/PHOTOTAKE.

DID YOU KNOW?

Ridding your puppy of worms is VERY IMPORTANT because certain worms that puppies carry can infect humans, such as tapeworms, hookworms and roundworms.

Since puppies are never housebroken at two to three weeks of age, it is easy for them to pass on the parasites (worms) to humans.

Breeders initiate a deworming programme two weeks after weaning. The routine is repeated every two or three weeks until the puppy is three months old. The breeder from whom you obtained your puppy should provide you with the complete details of the deworming programme.

Your veterinary surgeon can prescribe and monitor the programme of deworming for you. The usual programme is treating the puppy every 15–20 days until the puppy is positively worm free.

It is not advised that you treat your puppy with drugs which are not recommended professionally.

Male and female hookworms, *Ancylostoma caninum*, are uncommonly found in pet or show dogs in Britain. Hookworms may infect other dogs that have exposure to grasslands

The roundworm *Rhabditis*.

123

The infective stage of the hookworm larva.

(smart parasite!), it can be the cause of a very serious liver disease for humans. About 50 percent of the humans infected with *Echinococcus multilocularis*, causing alveolar hydatis, perish.

HEARTWORMS

Heartworms are thin, extended worms up to 30 cms. (12 ins.) long which live in a dog's heart and the major blood vessels around it. Staffordshires may have up to 200 of these worms. The symptoms may be loss of energy, loss of appetite, coughing, the development of a pot belly and anaemia.

Heartworms are transmitted by mosquitoes. The mosquito drinks the blood of an infected dog and takes in larvae with the blood. The larvae, called microfilaria, develop within the body of the mosquito and are passed on to the next dog bitten after the larvae mature. It takes two to three weeks for the larvae to develop to the infective stage within the body of the mosquito. Dogs should be treated at about six weeks of age, then every six months.

Blood testing for heartworms is not necessarily indicative of how seriously your dog is infected. This is a dangerous disease. Dogs in the United Kingdom are not affected by heartworm, although it is common in the U.S., Central Europe, Asia and Africa.

The head and rostellum (the round prominence on the scolex) of a tapeworm, which infects dogs and humans.

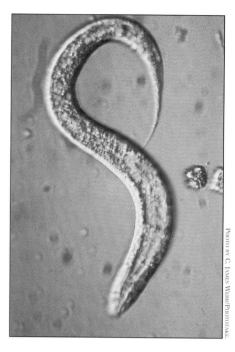

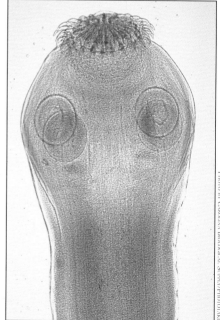

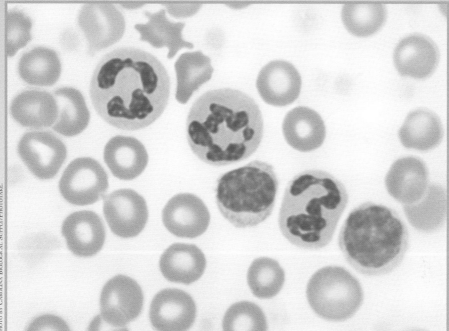

Magnified
heartworm
larvae,
*Dirofilaria
immitis.*

The heart
of a dog infected
with canine
heartworm,
*Dirofilaria
immitis.*

First Aid
at a Glance

Burns
Place the affected area under cool water; use ice if only a small area is burnt.

Bee/Insect bites
Apply ice to relieve swelling; antihistamine dosed properly.

Animal bites
Clean any bleeding area; apply pressure until bleeding subsides; go to the vet.

Spider bites
Use cold compress and a pressurised pack to inhibit venom's spreading.

Antifreeze poisoning
Immediately induce vomiting by using hydrogen peroxide.

Fish hooks
Removal best handled by vet; hook must be cut in order to remove.

Snake bites
Pack ice around bite; contact vet quickly; identify snake for proper antivenin.

Car accident
Move dog from roadway with blanket; seek veterinary aid.

Shock
Calm the dog, keep him warm; seek immediate veterinary help.

Nosebleed
Apply cold compress to the nose; apply pressure to any visible abrasion.

Bleeding
Apply pressure above the area; treat wound by applying a cotton pack.

Heat stroke
Submerge dog in cold bath; cool down with fresh air and water; go to the vet.

Frostbite/Hypothermia
Warm the dog with a warm bath, electric blankets or hot water bottles.

Abrasions
Clean the wound and wash out thoroughly with fresh water; apply antiseptic.

Remember: an injured dog may attempt to bite a helping hand from fear and confusion. Always muzzle the dog before trying to offer assistance.

YOUR SENIOR

Staffordshire Bull Terrier

The term old is a qualitative term. For dogs, as well as their masters, old is relative. Certainly we can all distinguish between a puppy Staffordshire and an adult Staffordshire—there are the obvious physical traits, such as size, appearance and facial expressions, as well as personality traits. Puppies that are nasty are very rare. Puppies and young dogs like to play with children. Children's natural exuberance is a good match for the seemingly endless energy of young dogs. They like to run, jump, chase and retrieve.

DID YOU KNOW?

The bottom line is simply that a dog is getting old when YOU think it is getting old because it slows down in its general activities, including walking, running, eating, jumping and retrieving. On the other hand, certain activities increase, like more sleeping, more barking and more repetition of habits like going to the door when you put your coat on without being called.

When dogs grow up and cease their interaction with children, they are often thought of as being too old to play with the kids.

On the other hand, if a Staffordshire is only exposed to people over 60 years of age, its

As Staffs become older, the hair around their mouths turns grey. This is usually the onset of the old age syndrome.

life will normally be less active and it will not seem to be getting old as its activity level slows down.

If people live to be 100 years old, dogs live to be 20 years old. While this is a good rule of thumb, it is VERY inaccurate. When trying to compare dog years to human years, you cannot make a generalisation about all

DID YOU KNOW?

An old dog starts to show one or more of the following symptoms:

• The hair on its face and paws starts to turn grey. The colour breakdown usually starts around the eyes and mouth.

• Sleep patterns are deeper and longer and the old dog is harder to awaken.

• The exercise routine becomes more and more tedious and the dog almost refuses to join exercises that it previously enjoyed.

• Food intake diminishes.

• Responses to calls, whistles and other signals are ignored more and more.

• Eye contacts do not evoke tail wagging (assuming they once did).

dogs. You can make the generalisation that 13 years is a good life span for a Staffordshire, compared to some of the Staffordshire's bull and mastiff cousins that scarcely live past 8 or 9 years. Dogs are generally considered mature within three years but they can reproduce even earlier. So the first three years of a dog's life are like seven times that of comparable humans. That means a three-year-old dog is like a 21-year-old person. As the curve of comparison shows, there is no hard and fast rule for comparing dog and human ages. The comparison is made even more difficult, for not all humans age at the same rate...and human females live longer than human males.

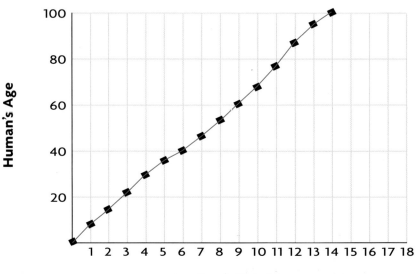

Human's Age vs **Dog's Age**

WHAT TO LOOK FOR IN SENIORS

Most veterinary surgeons and behaviourists use the seventh year mark as the time to consider a dog a 'senior.' The term 'senior' does not imply that the dog is geriatric and has begun to fail in mind and body. Ageing is essentially a slowing process. Humans readily admit that they feel a difference in their activity level from age 20 to 30, and then from 30 to 40, etc. By treating the seven-year-old dog as a senior, owners are able to implement certain therapeutic and preventive medical strategies with the help of their veterinary surgeons. A senior-care programme should

DID YOU KNOW?

The symptoms listed below are symptoms that gradually appear and become more noticeable. They are not life threatening; however, the symptoms below are to be taken very seriously and a discussion with your veterinary surgeon is warranted:

• Your dog cries and whimpers when it moves and stops running completely.

• Convulsions start or become more serious and frequent. The usual convulsion (spasm) is when the dog stiffens and starts to tremble, being unable or unwilling to move. The seizure usually lasts for 5 to 30 minutes.

• More and more toilet accidents occur. Urine and bowel movements take place indoors without warning.

• Vomiting becomes more and more frequent.

include at least two veterinary visits per year, screening sessions to determine the dog's health status, as well as nutritional counselling. Veterinary surgeons determine the senior dog's health status through a blood smear for a complete blood count, serum chemistry profile with electrolytes, urinalysis, blood pressure check, electrocardiogram, ocular tonometry (pressure on the eyeball), and dental prophylaxis.

Such an extensive programme for senior dogs is

Staffs normally live for 13 years, but dogs which have been properly fed and exercised can often exceed this.

129

well advised before owners start to see the obvious physical signs of ageing, such as slower and inhibited movement, greying, increased sleep/nap periods, and disinterest in play and other activity. This preventative programme promises a longer, healthier life for the ageing dog. Amongst the physical problems common in ageing dogs are the loss of sight and vision, arthritis, kidney and liver failure,

DID YOU KNOW?

Your senior dog may lose interest in eating, not because he's less hungry but because his senses of smell and taste have diminished. The old chow simply does not smell as good as it once did. Additionally, older dogs use less energy and thereby can sustain themselves on less food.

diabetes mellitus, heart disease, and Cushing's disease (a hormonal disease).

In addition to the physical manifestations discussed, there are some behavioural changes and problems related to ageing dogs. Dogs suffering from hearing or vision loss, dental discomfort or arthritis can become aggressive. Likewise the near-deaf and/or blind dog may be startled

more easily and react in an unexpectedly aggressive manner. Seniors suffering from senility can become more impatient and irritable. Housesoiling accidents are associated with loss of mobility, kidney problems, loss of sphincter control as well as plaque accumulation, physiological brain changes, and reactions to medications. Older dogs, just like young puppies, suffer from separation anxiety, which can lead to excessive barking, whining, housesoiling, and destructive behaviour. Seniors may become fearful of everyday sounds, such as vacuum cleaners, heaters, thunder, and passing traffic. Some dogs have difficulty sleeping, due to discomfort, the need for frequent potty visits, and the like. Owners should avoid spoiling the older dog with too many fatty treats. Obesity is a common problem in older dogs and subtracts years from their lifespan. Keep the senior dog as trim as possible since excessive weight puts additional stress on the body's vital organs. Some breeders recommend supplementing the diet with foods high in fibre and lower in calories. Adding fresh vegetables and marrow broth to the senior's diet makes a tasty, low-calorie, low-fat supplement. Vets also offer specialty diets for senior dogs that are worth exploring.

CDS: COGNITIVE DYSFUNCTION SYNDROME
"Old Dog Syndrome"

There are many ways to evaluate old-dog syndrome. Veterinary surgeons have defined CDS (cognitive dysfunction syndrome) as the gradual deterioration of cognitive abilities. These are indicated by changes in the dog's behaviour. When a dog changes its routine response, and maladies have been eliminated as the cause of these behavioural changes, then CDS is the usual diagnosis.

More than half the dogs over 8 years old suffer some form of CDS. The older the dog, the more chance it has of suffering from CDS. In humans, doctors often dismiss the CDS behavioural changes as part of 'winding down.'

There are four major signs of CDS: frequent toilet accidents inside the home, sleeps much more or much less than normal, acts confused, and fails to respond to social stimuli.

SYMPTOMS OF CDS

FREQUENT TOILET ACCIDENTS
- *Urinates in the house.*
- *Defecates in the house.*
- *Doesn't signal that he wants to go out.*

SLEEP PATTERNS
- *Moves much more slowly.*
- *Sleeps more than normal during the day.*
- *Sleeps less during the night.*
- *Walks around listlessly and without a destination goal.*

CONFUSION
- *Goes outside and just stands there.*
- *Appears confused with a faraway look in his eyes.*
- *Hides more often.*
- *Doesn't recognise friends.*
- *Doesn't come when called.*

FAILS TO RESPOND TO SOCIAL STIMULI
- *Comes to people less frequently, whether called or not.*
- *Doesn't tolerate petting for more than a short time.*
- *Doesn't come to the door when you return home from work.*

Your dog, as he nears his twilight years, needs his owner's patience and good care more than ever. Never punish an older dog for an accident or abnormal behaviour. For all the years of love, protection and companionship that your dog has provided, he deserves special attention and courtesies. The older dog may need to relieve himself at 3 a.m. because he can no longer hold it for eight hours. Older dogs may not be able to remain crated for more than two or three hours. It may be time to give up a sofa or chair to your old friend. Although he may not seem as enthusiastic about your attention and petting, he does appreciate the considerations you offer as he gets older.

Your Staffordshire does not understand why his world is slowing down. Owners must make the transition into the golden years as pleasant and rewarding as possible.

WHAT TO DO WHEN THE TIME COMES

You are never fully prepared to make a rational decision about putting your dog to sleep. It is very obvious that you love your Staffordshire or you would not be reading this book. Putting a loved dog to sleep is extremely difficult. It is a decision that must be made with your veterinary surgeon. You are usually forced to make the decision when one of the life-threatening symptoms listed above becomes serious enough for you to seek medical (veterinary) help.

If the prognosis of the malady indicates the end is near and your beloved pet will only suffer more and experience no enjoyment for the balance of its life, then euthanasia is the right choice.

WHAT IS EUTHANASIA?

Euthanasia derives from the Greek meaning good death. In other words, it means the planned, painless killing of a dog suffering from a painful, incurable condition, or who is so aged that it cannot walk, see, eat or control its excretory functions.

Euthanasia is usually accomplished by injection with an overdose of an anaesthesia or barbiturate. Aside from the prick of the needle, the experience is painless.

HOW ABOUT YOU?

The decision to euthanize your dog is hard. The days during which the dog becomes ill and the end occurs can be unusually stressful for you. If this is your first experience with the death of a loved one, you may need the comfort dictated by your religious beliefs. If you are the head of the family and have children, you should have

DID YOU KNOW?
Euthanasia must be done by a licensed veterinary surgeon. There also may be societies for the prevention of cruelty to animals in your area. They often offer this service upon a vet's recommendation.

involved them in the decision of putting your Staffordshire to sleep. Usually your dog can be maintained on drugs for a few days while it is kept in the clinic in order to give you ample time to make a decision. During this time, talking with members of the family or religious representatives, or even people who have lived through this same experience, can ease the burden of your inevitable decision. In any case, euthanasia is painful and stressful for the family of the dog. Unfortunately, it does not end there.

THE FINAL RESTING PLACE
Dogs can have the same privileges as humans. They can be buried in a pet cemetery in a burial container (very expensive); buried in your garden in a place suitably marked with a stone,

newly planted tree or bush; cremated with the ashes being given to you; or even stuffed and mounted by a taxidermist.

All of these options should be discussed frankly and openly with your veterinary surgeon. Do not be afraid to ask financial questions. Cremations are usually mass burnings and the ashes you get may not be only the ashes of your beloved dog. If you want a private cremation, there are very small crematoriums available to all veterinary clinics. Your vet can usually arrange for this but it may be a little more expensive.

A resting place for your dog's ashes may be available locally. Contact your veterinary surgeon or local dog club for more information.

GETTING ANOTHER DOG
The grief of losing your beloved dog will be as lasting as the grief of losing a human friend or relative. You cannot go out and buy another grandfather, but you can go out and buy another Staffordshire. In most cases, if your dog died of old age (if there is such a thing), it had slowed

DID YOU KNOW?

There are two drugs specifically designed to treat mental problems in dogs. About 7 million dogs each year are destroyed because owners can no longer tolerate their dogs' behaviour, according to Nicholas Dodman, a specialist in animal behaviour at Tufts University in Massachusetts.

The first drug, Clomicalm, is prescribed for dogs suffering from 'separation anxiety,' which is said to cause them to react when left alone by barking, chewing their owners' belongings, drooling copiously, or defecating or urinating inside the home.

The second drug, Anipryl, is recommended for canine cognitive dysfunction or 'old dog syndrome,' a mental deterioration that comes with age. Such dogs often seem to forget that they were housebroken, where their food bowls are, and they may even fail to recognise their owners.

A tremendous human-animal-bonding relationship is established with all dogs, particularly senior dogs. This precious relationship deteriorates when the dog does not recognise his master. The drug can restore the bond and make senior dogs feel more like their old selves.

down considerably. Do you want a new Staffordshire puppy to replace it? Or are you better off in finding a more mature Staffordshire, say two to three years of age, which will usually be housetrained and will have an already developed personality. In this case, you can find out if you like each other after a few hours of being together.

The decision is, of course, your own. Do you want another Staffordshire? Perhaps you want a smaller or larger dog? How much do you want to spend on a dog? Look in your local newspa-

pers for advertisements (DOGS FOR SALE), or, better yet, consult your local society for the prevention of cruelty to animals to adopt a dog. It is harder to find puppies at an animal shelter, but there are often many adult dogs in need of new homes. You may be able to find another

DID YOU KNOW?
The more open discussion you have about the whole stressful occurrence, the easier it will be for you when the time comes.

Staffordshire, or you may choose another breed or a mixed-breed dog. Private dog kennels specialising in a particular breed are the source for high-quality dogs that they usually breed from champion stock.

Whatever you decide, do it as quickly as possible. Most people usually buy the same breed because they know (and love) the characteristics of that breed. Then, too, they often know people who have the same breed and perhaps they are lucky enough that one of their friends expects a litter soon. What could be better?

If you are interested in burying your dog, there are pet cemeteries catering to pet lovers.

Many owners of Staffordshire Bull Terriers replace their dogs with new Staff puppies. The period of mourning and waiting varies from person to person. If the lost dog was a child's pet, it's advisable to replace it as soon as possible.

135

SHOWING YOUR
Staffordshire Bull Terrier

Is the puppy you selected growing into a handsome representative of his breed? You are rightly proud of your handsome little tyke, and he has mastered nearly all of the basic obedience commands that you have taught him. How about attending a dog show and seeing how the other half of the dog-loving world lives! Even if you never imagined yourself standing in the centre ring at the Crufts Dog Show, why not dream a little?

The first concept that the canine novice learns when watching a dog show is that each breed first competes against members of its own breed. Once the judge has selected the best member of each breed, then that chosen dog will compete with other dogs in its group. Finally the best of each group will compete for Best in Show and Reserve Best in Show.

The second concept that you must understand is that the dogs are not actually competing with one another. The judge compares each dog against the breed standard, which is a written description of the ideal

specimen of the breed. This imaginary dog never walked into a show ring, has never been bred and, to the woe of dog breeders around the globe, does not exist. Breeders attempt to get as close to this ideal as possible, with every litter, but theoretically the 'perfect' dog is so elusive that it is impossible. (And if the 'perfect' dog were born, breeders and judges would never agree that it was indeed 'perfect.')

If you are interested in exploring dog shows, your best

bet is to join your local breed club. These clubs host shows (often matches and open shows for beginners), send out newsletters, offer training days and provide an outlet to meet members who are often friendly and generous with their advice and contacts. To locate the nearest breed club for you, contact The Kennel Club, the ruling body for the British dog world. The Kennel Club governs not only conformation shows, but also working trials, obedience trials, agility trials and field trials. The Kennel Club furnishes the rules and regulations for all these events plus general dog registration and other basic requirements of dog ownership. Its annual show, held in

If you are going to show your dog, you must learn how to stand the dog in a pose that presents his best attributes.

Birmingham, is the largest bench show in England. Every year no fewer than 20,000 of the U.K.'s best dogs qualify to participate in this marvelous show that lasts four days.

The Kennel Club governs many different kinds of shows in Great Britain, Australia, South Africa and beyond. At the most competitive and prestigious of these shows, the Championship Shows, a dog can earn Challenge Certificates, and thereby become a 'champion.' A dog must earn three Challenge Certificates under three different judges to earn the prefix of 'Sh Ch' or 'Ch.' Some breeds must qualify in a field trial in order to gain the title of full champion. Challenge

WINNING THE TICKET

Earning a championship at Kennel Club shows is the most difficult in the world. Compared to the United States and Canada where it is relatively not 'challenging,' collecting three green tickets not only requires much time and effort, it can be very expensive! Challenge Certificates, as the tickets are properly known, are the building blocks of champions— good breeding, good handling, good training and good luck!

137

Certificates are awarded to a very small percentage of the dogs competing. The number of Challenge Certificates awarded in any one year is based upon the total number of dogs in each breed entered for competition. There are three types of

DID YOU KNOW?

Just like with anything else, there is a certain etiquette to the show ring that can only be learned through experience. Showing your dog can be quite intimidating to you as a novice when it seems as if everyone else knows what he's doing. You can familiarise yourself with ring procedure beforehand by taking a class to prepare you and your dog for conformation showing or by talking with an experienced handler. When you are in the ring, listen and pay attention to the judge and follow his/her directions. Remember, even the most skilled handlers had to start somewhere. Keep it up and you too will become a proficient handler before too long!

Championship Shows, a general show, where all breeds recognised by The Kennel Club can enter, a Group Show, and a breed show, which is limited to a single breed.

Open Shows are generally less competitive and are frequently used as 'practice shows' for young dogs. There are hundreds of Open Shows each year that can be invitingly social events and are great first show experiences for the novice. Even if you're just considering watching a show to wet your paws, an Open Show is a great choice.

While Championship and Open Shows are most important for the beginner to understand, there are other types of shows in which the interested dog owner can participate. Training clubs sponsor Matches that can be entered on the day of the show for a nominal fee. In these introductory-level exhibitions, two dogs are pulled from a raffle and 'matched,' the winner of that match goes on to the next round, and eventually only one dog is left undefeated.

Exemption shows are similar in that they are simply fun classes and usually held in conjunction with small agricultural shows. Primary shows can also be entered on the day of the event and dogs entered must not have won anything towards their titles. Sanction and Limited shows must be entered well in advance, and there are limitations upon who can enter. Regardless of which type you choose, you and your dog will have a grand time competing and learning your way about the shows.

Before you actually step into the ring, you would be well advised to sit back and observe the judge's ring procedure. If it is your first time in the ring, do not be over-anxious and run to the front of the line. It is much better to stand back and study how the exhibitor in front of you is performing. The judge asks each handler to 'stand' the dog, hopefully showing the dog off to his best advantage. The judge will observe the dog from a distance and, from different angles, approach the dog, check his teeth, overall structure, alertness and muscle tone, and consider how well the dog 'conforms' to the standard. Most importantly, the judge will have the exhibitor move the dog around the ring in some pattern that he or she should specify (another advantage to not going first, but always listen since some judges change their directions, and the judge is always right!) Finally the judge will give the dog one

Do not expect to take up a ribbon at your first show or trial. Be patient and continue to work with your dog every day.

last look before moving on to the next exhibitor.

If you are not in the top three at your first show, do not be discouraged. Be patient and consistent and you will eventually find yourself in the winning lineup. Remember that the winners were once in your shoes and have devoted many hours and much money to earn the placement. If you find that your dog is losing every time and never getting a nod, it may be time to consider a different dog sport or just enjoy your Staffordshire as a pet.

WORKING TRIALS
Working trials can be entered by any well-trained dog of any breed, not just Gundogs or Working dogs. Many dogs that earn the Kennel Club Good

---

DID YOU KNOW?

The Kennel Club divides its dogs into seven Groups: Gundogs, Utility, Working, Toy, Terrier, Hounds and Pastoral.*

*The Pastoral Group, established in 1999, includes those sheepdog breeds previously categorised in the Working Group.

DID YOU KNOW?
You can get information about dog shows from kennel clubs and breed clubs:

Fédération Cynologique Internationale
14, rue Leopold II, B-6530 Thuin, Belgium
www.fci.be

The Kennel Club
1-5 Clarges St., Piccadilly, London W1Y 8AB, UK
www.the-kennel-club.org.uk

American Kennel Club
5580 Centerview Drive
Raleigh, NC 27606-3390, USA
www.akc.org

Canadian Kennel Club
89 Skyway Ave., Suite 100, Etobicoke
Ontario M9W 6R4 Canada
www.ckc.ca

At the CD stake, dogs must participate in four groups, Control, Stay, Agility and Search (Retrieve and Nosework). At the next three levels, UD, WD and TD, there are only three groups: Control, Agility and Nosework.

Agility consists of three jumps: a vertical scale up a six-foot wall of planks; a clear jump over a basic three-foot hurdle with a removable top bar; and a long jump across angled planks stretching nine feet.

To earn the UD, WD and TD, dogs must track approximately one-half mile for articles laid from one-half hour to

Citizen Dog award choose to participate in a working trial. There are five stakes at both open and championship levels: Companion Dog (CD), Utility Dog (UD), Working Dog (WD), Tracking Dog (TD), and Patrol Dog (PD). Like in conformation shows, dogs compete against a standard and if the dog reaches the qualifying mark, it obtains a certificate. Divided into groups, each exercise must be achieved 70 percent in order to qualify. If the dog achieves 80 percent in the open level, it receives a Certificate of Merit (COM), in the championship level, it receives a Qualifying Certificate.

CLASSES AT DOG SHOWS
There can be as many as 18 classes per sex for your breed. Check the show schedule carefully to make sure that you have entered your dog in the appropriate class. Among the classes offered can be: Beginners; Minor Puppy (ages 6 to 9 months); Puppy (ages 6 to 12 months); Junior (ages 6 to 18 months); Beginners (handler or dog never won first place) as well as the following, each of which is defined in the schedule: Maiden; Novice; Tyro; Debutant; Undergraduate; Graduate; Postgraduate; Minor Limit; Mid Limit; Limit; Open; Veteran; Stud Dog; Brood Bitch; Progeny; Brace and Team.

DID YOU KNOW?

The Kennel Club's Junior Organisation is a way for young people to enjoy training and participating in activities with their dogs while learning about showing and ring procedure. Through a variety of events on both local and national levels, Junior Organisation members between the ages of 8 and 18 are introduced to the dog sport and learn about responsible care of dogs, good sportsmanship and proper training, to name just a few of the benefits of membership. The Organisation is a wonderful opportunity for future handlers and young pet dog enthusiasts alike.

three hours ago. Tracks consist of turns and legs, and fresh ground is used for each participant.

The fifth stake, PD, involves teaching manwork, which is not recommended for every breed.

FIELD TRIALS AND WORKING TESTS

Working tests are frequently used to prepare dogs for field trials, the purpose of which is to heighten the instincts and natural abilities of gundogs. Live game is not used in working tests. Unlike field trials, working tests do not count toward a dog's record at The Kennel Club, though the same judges often oversee working tests. Field trials began

DOG SHOW DEFINITIONS

Following are definitions of some common dog show terminology:

Benched show: Show in which dogs must await their turn in the ring in a designated area; usually each dog is provided with an individual partitioned-off area in which to stay during the show.

Best in Show: Award given to the dog judged best of all entries among dogs of all breeds.

Best of Breed: Award given to the dog jugded best of all entries among dogs of the same breed.

Champion: Title given to a dog who has earned three Challenge Certificates under three different judges, plus has qualified in a working/field trial.

Conformation: How well the dog measures up to, or 'conforms' to, its particular breed standard.

Limited show: Show that is restricted to members of certain societies only.

Show Champion: Title given to a dog who has earned three Challenge Certificates under three different judges.

Stand: Posture in which the handler positions the dog for examination by the judge.

Staffordshire
Bull Terriers
usually do well
in agility trials
because they are
exceptionally
athletic and
always keen to
please.

in England in 1947 and are
only moderately popular among
dog folk. While breeders of
Working and Gundog breeds
concern themselves with the
field abilities of their dogs,
there is considerably less
interest in field trials than dog
shows. In order for dogs to
become full champions, certain
breeds must qualify in the field
as well. Upon gaining three CCs
in the show ring, the dog is
designated a Show Champion
(Sh Ch). The title Champion
(Ch) requires that the dog gain
an award at a field trial, be a

'special qualifier' at a field trial
or pass a 'special show dog
qualifier' judged by a field trial
judge on a shooting day.

AGILITY TRIALS
Agility trials began in the
United Kingdom in 1977 and
have since spread around the
world, especially to the United
States, where it enjoys strong
popularity. The handler directs
his dog over an obstacle course
that includes jumps (such as
those used in the working
trials), as well as tyres, the dog
walk, weave poles, pipe tunnels,

HOW TO ENTER A DOG SHOW
1. Obtain an entry form and show schedule from the Show Secretary.
2. Select the classes that you want to enter and complete the entry form.
3. Transfer your dog into your name at The Kennel Club. (Be sure that this matter is handled before entering.)
4. Find out how far in advance show entries must be made. Oftentimes it's more than a couple of months.

collapsed tunnels, etc. The Kennel Club requires that dogs not be trained for agility until they are 12 months old. This dog sport intends to be great fun and interested owners should join a training club that has obstacles and experienced agility handlers who can introduce you and your dog to the 'ropes' (and tyres, tunnels and so on).

FÉDÉRATION CYNOLOGIQUE INTERNATIONALE
Established in 1911, the Fédération Cynologique Internationale represents the 'world kennel club.' This international body brings uniformity to the breeding, judging and showing of purebred dogs. Although the FCI originally included only four European nations: France, Holland, Austria and Belgium (which remains its headquarters), the organisation today embraces nations on six continents and

recognises well over 400 breeds of purebred dog. There are three titles attainable through the FCI: the International Champion, which is the most prestigious; the International Beauty Champion, which is based on aptitude certificates in different countries; and the International Trial Champion, which is based on achievement in obedience trials in different countries. Quarantine laws in England and Australia prohibit most of their exhibitors from entering FCI shows.The rest of the European Union do participate in these impressive canine spectacles, the largest of which is the World Dog Show, hosted in a different country each year. FCI sponsors both national and international shows. The hosting country determines the judging system and breed standards are always based on the breed's country of origin.

DID YOU KNOW?
The Kennel Club's Good Citizen programme is the largest training programme in the U.K. It is for all dogs, purebred and mixed breed, and its goal is to promote the responsible training, ownership and care of dogs.

The scheme is divided into three levels: Bronze, Silver and Gold. It is more than just training; it is a total programme that focuses on every aspect of dog ownership.

Staffordshire Bull Terrier

As a Staffordshire owner, you have selected your dog so that you and your loved ones can have a companion, a protector, a friend and a four-legged family member. You invest time, money and effort to care for and train the family's new charge. Of course, this chosen canine behaves perfectly! Well, perfectly like a dog.

THINK LIKE A DOG

Dogs do not think like humans, nor do humans think like dogs, though we try. Unfortunately, a dog is incapable of figuring out how humans think, so the responsibility falls on the owner to adopt a proper

DID YOU KNOW?

Physical games like pulling contests, wrestling, jumping and teasing should not be encouraged. Inciting the dog's crazy behaviour tends to confuse a dog. The owner has to be able to control his dog at all times; even in play, your dog has to know you're the leader and you decide when to play and when to behave mannerly.

canine mindset. Dogs cannot rationalise, and dogs exist in the present moment. Many dog owners make the mistake in training of thinking that they can reprimand their dog for something he did a while ago. Basically, you cannot even reprimand a dog for something he did 20 seconds ago! Either catch him in the act or forget it! It is a waste of your and your dog's time—in his mind, you are reprimanding him for whatever he is doing at that moment.

The following behavioural problems represent some which owners most commonly encounter. Every dog is unique and every situation is unique. No author could purport to solve your Staffordshire's problem simply by reading a script. Here we outline some basic 'dogspeak' so that owners' chances of solving behavioural problems are increased. Discuss bad habits with your veterinary surgeon and he/she can recommend a behavioural specialist to consult in appropriate cases. Since behavioural abnormalities are the leading reason owners abandon their pets, we hope that you will make a valiant effort to solve your

Staffordshire's problem. Patience and understanding are virtues that dwell in every pet-loving household.

AGGRESSION
This is the most obvious problem that concerns owners of Staffordshire Bull Terriers. Aggression can be a very big problem in dogs, but more so in a dog with a fighting background. Aggression, when not controlled, always becomes dangerous. An aggressive dog, no matter the size, may lunge at, bite or even attack a person or another dog. Aggressive behaviour is not to be tolerated. It is more than just inappropriate behaviour; it is not safe, especially with a tenacious, powerful breed such as the Staffordshire. It is painful for a family to watch their dog become unpredictable in his behaviour to the point where they are afraid of him. While not all aggressive behaviour is dangerous, growling, baring teeth, etc., can be frightening: It is important to ascertain why the dog is acting in this manner. Aggression is a display of dominance, and the dog

> **DID YOU KNOW?**
> Dog aggression is a serious problem. NEVER give an aggressive dog to someone else. The dog will usually be more aggressive in a new situation where his leadership is unchallenged and unquestioned (in his mind).

> **DID YOU KNOW?**
> DANGER! If you and your on-lead dog are approached by a larger, running dog that is not restrained, walk away from the dog as quickly as possible. Don't allow your dog to make eye contact with the other dog. You should not make eye contact either. In dog terms, eye contact indicates a challenge.

should not have the dominant role in its pack, which is, in this case, your family.

It is important not to challenge an aggressive dog as this could provoke an attack. Observe your

Dogs should be tethered when first introduced. Some Staffs become aggressive when their leadership is challenged.

Staffordshire's body language. Does he make direct eye contact and stare? Does he try to make himself as large as possible: ears pricked, chest out, tail erect? Height and size signify authority in a dog pack—being taller or 'above' another dog literally means that he is 'above' in the social status. These body signals tell you that your Staffordshire thinks he is in charge, a problem that needs to be addressed. An aggressive dog is

145

DID YOU KNOW?

DID YOU KNOW?
Your dog inherited the pack-leader mentality. He only knows about pecking order. He instinctively wants to be top dog but you have to convince him that you are boss. There is no such thing as living in a democracy with your dog. You are the dictator, the absolute monarch.

unpredictable. You never know when he is going to strike and what he is going to do. You cannot understand why a dog that is playful and loving one minute is growling and snapping the next.

The best solution is to consult a behavioural specialist, one who has experience with the Staffordshire if possible. Together, perhaps you can pinpoint the cause of your dog's aggression and do something about it. An aggressive dog cannot be trusted, and a dog that cannot be trusted is not safe to have as a family pet. If the pet Staffordshire becomes untrustworthy, he cannot be kept in the home with the family. The family must get rid of the dog. In the worst case, the dog must be euthanised.

AGGRESSION TOWARD OTHER DOGS

In general, a dog's aggressive behaviour toward another dog stems from not enough exposure to other dogs at an early age. In Staffordshires, early socialisation with other dogs is absolutely

Play between dogs rarely turns into aggression. This dam is playing with her pup while teaching it the difference between roughhouse playing and true aggression.

essential. Staffordshires are naturally aggressive toward other dogs: they were bred to be 'anti-dog.' It's the breeder and owner's responsibility to curb and redirect this aggression so that the Staffordshire can become an upright member of canine society. If other dogs make your Staffordshire nervous and agitated, he will lash out as a defensive mechanism. A dog who has not received sufficient exposure to other canines tends to believe that he is the only dog on the planet. The animal becomes so dominant that he does not even show signs that he is fearful or threatened. Without growling or any other physical signal as a warning, he will lunge at and bite the other dog. A way to correct this is to let your Staffordshire approach another dog when walking on lead. Watch very closely and at the very first sign of aggression, correct your Staffordshire and pull him away. Scold him for any sign of discomfort, and then praise him when he ignores or tolerates the other dog. Keep this up until ho

stops the aggressive behaviour, learns to ignore the other dog or even accepts other dogs. Praise him lavishly for his correct behaviour.

DOMINANT AGGRESSION

A social hierarchy is firmly established in a wild dog pack. The dog wants to dominate those under him and please those above him. Dogs know that there must be a leader. If you are not the obvious choice for emperor, the dog will assume the throne! These conflicting innate desires are what a dog owner is up against when he sets about training a dog. In training a dog to obey commands, the owner is reinforcing that he is the top dog in the 'pack' and that the dog should, and should want to, serve his superior. Thus, the owner is suppressing the dog's urge to dominate by modifying his behaviour and making him obedient.

An important part of training is taking every opportunity to reinforce that you are the leader. The simple action of making your Staffordshire sit to wait for his food instead of allowing him to run up to get it when he wants it says that you control when he eats and that he is dependent on you for food. Although it may be difficult, do not give in to your dog's wishes every time he whines at you or looks at you

> **DID YOU KNOW?**
>
> Dogs and humans may be the only animals that smile. Dogs imitate the smile on their owner's face when he greets a friend. The dog only smiles
>
>
>
> at its human friends. It never smiles at another dog or cat. Usually it rolls up its lips and shows its teeth in a clenched mouth while it rolls over onto its back begging for a soft scratch.

with pleading eyes. It is a constant effort to show the dog that his place in the pack is at the bottom. This is not meant to sound cruel or inhumane. You love your Staffordshire and you should treat him with care and affection. You (hopefully) did not get a dog just so you could boss around another creature. Dog training is not about being cruel or feeling important, it is about moulding the dog's behaviour into what is acceptable and teaching him to live by your rules. In theory, it is quite simple: catch him in appropriate

DID YOU KNOW?

Males, whether castrated or not, will mount almost anything: a pillow, your leg or, much to your horror, even your neighbour's leg. As with other types of inappropriate behaviour, the dog must be corrected while in the act, which for once is not difficult. Often he will not let go! While a puppy is experimenting with his very first urges, his owners feel he needs to 'sow his oats' and allow the pup to mount. As the pup grows into a full-size dog, with full-size urges, it becomes a nuisance and an embarrassment. Males always appear as if they are trying to 'save the race,' more determined and stronger than imaginable. While altering the dog at an appropriate age will limit the dog's desire, it usually does not remove it entirely.

behaviour and reward him for it. Add a dog into the equation and it becomes a bit more trying, but as a rule of thumb, positive reinforcement is what works best.

With a dominant dog, punishment and negative reinforcement can have the opposite effect of what you are after. It can make a dog fearful and/or act out aggressively if he feels he is being challenged. Remember, a dominant dog perceives himself at the top of the social heap and will fight to defend his perceived status. The best way to prevent that is never

to give him reason to think that he is in control in the first place. If you are having trouble training your Staffordshire and it seems as if he is constantly challenging your authority, seek the help of an obedience trainer or behavioural specialist. A professional will work with both you and your dog to teach you effective techniques to use at home. Beware of trainers who rely on excessively harsh methods; scolding is necessary now and then, but the focus in your training should always be on positive reinforcement.

If you can isolate what brings out the fear reaction, you can help the dog get over it. Supervise your Staffordshire's interactions with people and other dogs, and praise the dog when it goes well. If he starts to act aggressively in a situation, correct him and remove him from the situation. Do not let people approach the dog and start petting him without your express permission. That way, you can have the dog sit to accept petting, and praise him when he behaves properly. You are focusing on praise and on modifying his behaviour by rewarding him when he acts appropriately. By being gentle and by supervising his interactions, you are showing him that there is no need to be afraid or defensive.

SEXUAL BEHAVIOUR

Dogs exhibit certain sexual behaviours that may have influenced your choice of male or female when you first purchased your Staffordshire. Spaying/neutering will eliminate these behaviours, but if you are purchasing a dog that you wish to breed, you should be aware of what you will have to deal with throughout the dog's life.

Female dogs usually have two oestruses per year with each season lasting about three weeks. These are the only times in which a female dog will mate, and she usually will not allow this until the second week of the cycle. If a bitch is not bred during the heat cycle, it is not uncommon for her to experience a false pregnancy, in which her mammary glands swell and she exhibits maternal tendencies toward toys or other objects.

Owners must further recognise that mounting is not merely a sexual expression but also one of dominance. Be consistent and persistent and you will find that you can 'move mounters.'

CHEWING

The national canine pastime is chewing! Every dog loves to sink his 'canines' into a tasty bone, but sometimes that bone is attached to his owner's hand! Dogs need to chew, to massage their gums, to

Staffordshire Bull Terriers have strong jaws and teeth. They destroy most dog toys in short order. Use only toys made specifically for dogs, which are tougher and stronger.

DID YOU KNOW?

Fear in a grown dog is often the result of improper or incomplete socialisation as a pup, or it can be the result of a traumatic experience he suffered when young. Keep in mind that the term 'traumatic' is relative—something that you would not think twice about can leave a lasting negative impression on a puppy. If the dog experiences a similar experience later in life, he may try to fight back to protect himself. Again, this behaviour is very unpredictable, especially if you do not know what is triggering his fear.

Scratch his belly and watch him smile! Staffs have a real sense of humour.

make their new teeth feel better and to exercise their jaws. This is a natural behaviour deeply imbedded in all things canine. Our role as owners is not to stop chewing, but to redirect it to positive, chew-worthy objects. Be an informed owner and purchase proper chew toys like strong nylon bones made for large dogs for your Staffordshire. Be sure that the devices are safe and durable, since your dog's safety is at risk. Again, the owner is responsible for ensuring a dog-proof environment. The best answer is prevention: that is, put your shoes, handbags and other tasty objects in their proper places (out of the reach of the growing canine mouth). Direct puppies to their toys whenever you see them tasting the furniture legs or your pant leg. Make a loud noise to attract the pup's attention and immediately escort him to his chew toy and engage him with the toy for at least four minutes, praising and encouraging him all the while.

Some trainers recommend deterrents, such as hot pepper or another bitter spice or a product designed for this purpose, to discourage the dog from chewing on unwanted objects. This is sometimes reliable, though not as often as the manufacturers of such products claim. Test out the product with your own dog before investing in a case of it.

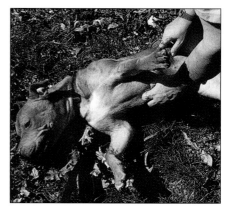

JUMPING UP
Jumping up is a dog's friendly way of saying hello! Some dog owners do not mind when their dog jumps up, which is fine for them. The problem arises when guests come to the house and the dog greets them in the same manner—whether they like it or not! However friendly the greeting may be, chances are your visitors will not appreciate being knocked over by your boisterous Staffordshire. The dog will not be able to distinguish upon whom he can jump and whom he cannot. Therefore, it is probably best to discourage this behaviour entirely.

Pick a command such as 'off' (avoid using 'down' since you will use that for the dog to lie down) and tell him 'off' when he jumps up. Place him on the ground on all fours and have him sit, praising him the whole time. Always lavish him with praise and petting when he is in the 'sit' position. That way you are still giving him a warm affectionate greeting, because you are as excited to see him as he is to see you!

DIGGING

Digging, which is seen as a destructive behaviour to humans, is actually quite a natural behaviour in dogs. Since your Staffordshire is one of the 'earth dogs' (also known as terriers), his desire to dig can be irrepressible and most frustrating to his owners. When digging occurs in your garden, it is actually a normal behaviour redirected into something the dog can do in his everyday life. In the wild a dog would be actively seeking food, making his own shelter, etc. He would be using his paws in a purposeful manner for his survival. Since you provide him with food and shelter, he has no need to use his paws for these purposes, and so the energy that he would be using manifests itself in the form of little holes all over your garden and flower beds.

Perhaps your dog is digging as a reaction to boredom—it is somewhat similar to someone eating a whole bag of pretzels in front of the Tele—because they are there and there is not anything better to do! Basically, the answer is to provide the dog with adequate play and exercise so that his mind and paws are occupied, and so that he feels as if he is doing something useful.

Of course, digging is easiest to control if it is stopped as soon as possible, but it is often hard to catch a dog in the act, especially if he is alone in the garden during the day. If your dog is a compulsive digger and is not easily distracted by other activities, you can designate an area on your property where it is okay for him to dig. If you catch him digging in an off-limits area of the garden, immediately bring him to the approved area and praise him for digging there. Keep a close eye on him so that you can catch him as that is the only way he is going to understand what is permitted and what is not. If you bring him to a hole he dug an hour ago and tell him 'No,' he will understand that you are not fond of holes, or dirt, or flowers. If you catch him while he is stifle-deep in your tulips, that is when he will get your message.

BARKING

Dogs cannot talk—oh, what they would say if they could! Instead, barking is a dog's way of 'talking.' It can be somewhat frustrating because it is not always easy to tell what a dog means by his bark—is he excited, happy, frightened or angry? Whatever it is that the dog is trying to say, he should not be punished for barking. Only when the barking becomes excessive, and when the excessive barking becomes a bad habit, does the behaviour need to be modified. Fortunately, Staffordshires are not as vocal as most other terriers, and they tend to use their barks more purposefully than most dogs. If an intruder came into your home in the middle of the night and your Staffordshire barked a warning, wouldn't you be pleased? You would probably deem your dog a hero, a wonderful guardian and protector of the home. Most dogs are not as discriminate as the Staffordshire. For instance, if a friend drops by unexpectedly and rings the doorbell and is greeted with a sudden sharp bark, you would probably be annoyed at the dog. But in reality, isn't this just the same behaviour? The dog does not know any better...unless he sees who is at the door and it is someone he knows, he will bark as a means of vocalising that his (and your) territory is being threatened. While your friend is not posing a threat, it is all the same to the dog. Barking is his means of letting you know that there is an intrusion, whether friend or foe, on your property. This type of barking is instinctive and should not be discouraged.

Excessive habitual barking, however, is a problem that should be corrected early on. As your Staffordshire grows up, you will be able to tell when his barking is purposeful and when it is for no reason. You will become able to distinguish your dog's different barks and their meanings. For example, the bark when someone comes to the door will be different from the bark when he is excited to see you. It is similar to a person's tone of voice, except that the dog has to rely totally on tone of voice because he does not have the benefit of using words. An incessant barker will be evident at an early age.

There are some things that encourage a dog to bark. For example, if your dog barks non-stop for a few minutes and you give him a treat to quiet him, he believes that you are rewarding him for barking. He will associate barking with getting a treat, and will keep doing it until he is rewarded.

FOOD STEALING

Is your dog devising ways of stealing food from your cupboard? If so, you must answer the following questions: Is your Staffordshire hungry, or is he 'constantly famished' like every other chow hound? Why is there food on the counter top? Face it, some dogs are more food-motivated than others; some dogs are totally obsessed by a slab of brisket and can only think of their next meal. Food stealing is terrific fun and always yields a great reward—FOOD, glorious food.

The owner's goal, therefore, is to make the 'reward' less rewarding, even startling! Plant a shaker can (an empty pop can with coins inside) on the counter so that it catches your pooch offguard. There are other devices available that will surprise the dog when he is looking for a mid-afternoon snack. Such remote-control devices, though not the first choice of some trainers, allow the correction to come from the object instead of the owner. These devices are also useful to keep the snacking hound from napping on furniture that is forbidden.

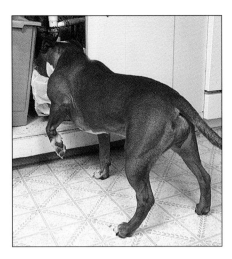

Begging and food stealing must never be tolerated from your dog. Your Staffordshire may be as clever and industrious as this fellow who's learned to open the pantry doors.

BEGGING

Just like food stealing, begging is a favourite pastime of hungry puppies! It yields that same reward—FOOD! Dogs quickly learn that their owners keep the 'good food' for themselves, and that we humans do not dine on kibble alone. Begging is a conditioned response related to a specific stimulus, time and place. The sounds of the kitchen, cans and bottles opening, crinkling bags, the smell of food in preparation, etc., will excite the chow hound and soon the paws are in the air!

Here is the solution to stopping this behaviour: Never give into a beggar! You are rewarding the dog for sitting pretty, jumping up, whining and rubbing his nose into you by giving him that glorious reward—food. By ignoring the dog, you will (eventu-

ally) force the behaviour into extinction. Note that the behaviour likely gets worse before it disappears, so be sure there are not any 'softies' in the family who will give in to little 'Oliver' every time he whimpers, 'More, please.'

SEPARATION ANXIETY

Your Staffordshire may howl, whine or otherwise vocalise his displeasure at your leaving the house and his being left alone. This is a normal case of separation anxiety, and there are things that can be done to eliminate this problem. Your dog needs to learn that he will be fine on his own for a while and that he will not wither away if he is not attended to every minute of the day. In fact, constant attention can lead to separation anxiety in the first place. If you are endlessly coddling and cooing over your dog, he will come to expect this from you all of the time and it will be more traumatic for him when you are not there. Obviously, you enjoy spending time with your dog, and he thrives on your love and attention. However, it should not become a dependent relationship where he is heartbroken without you.

One thing you can do to minimise separation anxiety is to make your entrances and exits as low-key as possible. Do not give your dog a long drawn-out goodbye, and do not lavish him with hugs and kisses when you return. This is giving in to the attention that he craves, and it will only make him miss it more when you are away. Another thing you can try is to give your dog a treat when you leave; this will not only keep him occupied and keep his mind off the fact that you just left, but it will also help him associate your leaving with a pleasant experience.

You may have to accustom your dog to being left alone in intervals, much like when you introduced your pup to his crate. Of course, when your dog starts whimpering as you approach the door, your first instinct will be to run to him and comfort him, but do not do it! Really—eventually he will adjust and be just fine if you take it in small steps. His anxiety stems from being placed in an unfamiliar situation; by familiarising him with being alone he will learn that he is okay. That is not to

DID YOU KNOW?
The number of dogs who suffer from separation anxiety is on the rise as more and more pet owners find themselves at work all day. New attention is being paid to this problem, which is especially hard to diagnose since it is only evident when the dog is alone. Research is currently being done to help educate dog owners about separation anxiety and about how they can help minimise this problem in their dogs.

say you should purposely leave your dog home alone, but the dog needs to know that while he can depend on you for his care, you do not have to be by his side 24 hours a day.

When the dog is alone in the house, he should be confined to his crate or a designated dog-proof area of the house. This should be the area in which he sleeps and already feels comfortable so he will feel more at ease when he is alone. This is just one of the many examples in which a crate is an invaluable tool for you and your dog, and another reinforcement of why your dog should view his crate as a 'happy' place, a place of his own.

COPROPHAGIA
Faeces eating is, to most humans, one of the most disgusting behaviours that their dog could

engage in, yet to the dog it is perfectly normal. It is hard for us to understand why a dog would want to eat its own faeces. He could be seeking certain nutrients that are missing from his diet; he could be just plain hungry; or he could be attracted by the pleasing (to a dog) scent. While coprophagia most often refers to the dog eating his own faeces, a dog may eat that of another animal as well if he comes across it. Vets have found that diets with a low digestibility, containing relatively low levels of fibre and high levels of starch, increase coprophagia. Therefore, high-fibre diets may decrease the likelihood of dogs' eating faeces. Both the consistency of the stool (how firm it feels in the dog's mouth) and the presence of undigested nutrients increase the likelihood. Dogs often find the stool of cats and horses more palatable than that of other dogs. Once the dog develops diarrhoea from faeces eating, it will likely quit this distasteful habit, since dogs tend to prefer eating harder faeces.

To discourage this behaviour, first make sure that the food you are feeding your dog is nutritionally complete and that he is getting enough food. If changes in his diet do not seem to work, and no medical cause can be found, you will have to modify the behaviour before it becomes a habit through environmental control. There are some tricks you can try, such as adding an unpleasant-tasting substance to the faeces to make them unpalatable or adding something to the dog's food which will make it unpleasant tasting after it passes through the dog. The best way to prevent your dog from eating his stool is to make it unavailable—clean up after he eliminates and remove any stool from the garden. If it is not there, he cannot eat it.

This Staff jumped up and stole the child's biscuit. Children should always be supervised when in the company of dogs, especially when the child has a sweet!

Never reprimand the dog for stool eating, as this rarely impresses the dog. Vets recommend distracting the dog while he is in the act of stool eating. Another option is to muzzle the dog when he is in the garden to relieve himself; this usually is effective within 30 to 60 days. Coprophagia is seen most frequently in pups 6 to 12 months of age and usually disappears around the dog's first birthday.

INDEX

Page numbers in **boldface** indicate illustrations.

My Staffordshire Bull Terrier

PUT YOUR PUPPY'S FIRST PICTURE HERE

Dog's Name ███████ ███████ ████ (█████)

Date _____ Photographer _____